Winter

Winter

ATLANTIC CANADIAN STORIES

Edited and with an
introduction by Dan Soucoup

NIMBUS
PUBLISHING LTD
nimbus.ca

Nimbus Publishing Limited
3731 Mackintosh St, Halifax, NS, B3K 5A5
(902) 455-4286 nimbus.ca

Printed and bound in Canada

NB1254

Cover design: Jenn Embree
Interior design: Grace Laemmler

Library and Archives Canada Cataloguing in Publication

Winter : Atlantic Canadian stories / edited by Dan Soucoup.

ISBN 978-1-77108-558-8 (softcover)

1. Winter—Canada—Literary collections. 2. Short stories, Canadian (English)—
Atlantic Provinces. 3. Canadian prose literature (English)—20th century. 4. Canadian
prose literature (English)—21st century. I. Soucoup, Dan, 1949-, editor

PS8323.W57W56 2017   C813'.010836   C2017-904101-0

Nimbus Publishing acknowledges the financial support for its publishing activities from the Government of Canada, the Canada Council for the Arts, and from the Province of Nova Scotia. We are pleased to work in partnership with the Province of Nova Scotia to develop and promote our creative industries for the benefit of all Nova Scotians.

CONTENTS

INTRODUCTION

It is April 16 and I am skiing a trail along the Kennetcook River in Nova Scotia's Hants County. With a metre of snow underfoot, it feels like February. I pass a frozen lake and six bewildered geese are standing on the ice wondering why they ever bothered flying back from Florida. A deer, no doubt very hungry, crosses the trail, and further along on a sidehill facing the noonday sun, brown dirt is poking through patches of snow where robins are desperately picking for nourishment. A strange, almost eternal winter is present. This seemingly never-ending season is upon us. And yet, this is Canada: a place where winter thrives—or at least reaches its apex. It is not for the faint of heart, but here I am in a fine state of affairs, gliding effortlessly across an ice-covered landscape in the glorious early spring sunshine.

Winter can no doubt be the cruellest time of year, when nature seems entirely indifferent to human concerns. Motorists get stranded in downtown streets, metre-high snowdrifts block one's way, and roofs cave in from the sheer volume of ice and snow. From November to April, snowstorms can occur with such frequency and severity that, for those unprepared or tending to procrastinate, it can be a time of great peril. Cold and murky, hard and enduring, our vision of the coldest season is not always pleasant. Winter's brutality gets ingrained into our minds and, as the brilliant writer Adam Gopnik remarked, winter comes to the northern hemisphere due to planetary tilt but in the darkest months, we view it as God's reprimand.

And who else can appreciate this strange situation? Russians, Scandinavians, and some Americans, but the vast majority of humans shudder at the prospect of spending six months in a deep freeze.

According to climatologists, Canada is the second-coldest land mass on the planet (after Antarctica) but "we the north" are number one in terms of snowfall.

Two remedies for the winter blues seem apparent. One is the combination of a snug chair, a book, and a roaring fire with snow falling gently outside. This remedy is certainly enhanced with family and friends nearby to help celebrate year's end. Another equally prevailing—but less romantic—remedy of the so-called "gloomy season" is the splendid winterfest of sports it offers. Hiking, skating, skiing, snowshoeing, snowmobiling, and, above all, hockey, grip Canadians in the winter months, and our passion for these outdoor activities does much to set us apart from our southern neighbours.

And so this collection from the Great White North offers readers stories of outdoor adventure—on rinks, across ice-covered ponds, and through forest trails—where the excitement of the bracing terrain is constantly present in all its sparkling, frosty wonder. As everyone who has experienced the numbing cold resulting from being outside too long knows, the winter months can be dangerous, even for hearty outdoor types.

Tapping into this paradox, Jim Lutes has written a remarkable account of skating across Nova Scotia one cold February day—and night. Not a writer by trade, Jim has succeeded in conveying that extraordinary sense of exhilaration and fear that accompanies one disoriented in the woods in the middle of winter. As well, a mysterious writer operating under the pen name "Steve Lance" provides an exciting and frightening account of being lost at night in the wilds of Nova Scotia's rugged Cape Chignecto region.

Paul Skerry has crafted a true story about an ill-fated ski trip into the wilds of Kejimkujik National Park. Despite an almost disastrous turn of events, the excursion later develops into an annual overnight trek into the frozen wilderness. In addition, outdoor adventure guide Scott Cunningham has written an exceptional description of a skiing trip across the rugged Cape Breton highlands one week in February. And Nova Scotia writer Sara Jewell has chronicled a thrilling story of two young boys on snowmobiles one starry evening. Speeding over icy terrain, the boys suddenly plunge through river ice and become trapped in freezing water.

From Thomas H. Raddall, one of Canada's finest writers, comes the amazing tale of courage and grit one winter's day in 1910 when a young widow becomes lost and disoriented in a blinding snowstorm on the ice-covered LaHave River in Nova Scotia. And from the eminent historic writer of seafaring classics, Archibald MacMechan, comes the tale of an impossible winter rescue on the high seas. Also Alistair MacLeod, one of our very best contemporary writers with a superb international reputation, has written an outstanding story of a courageous dog saving a young boy in the frozen ice floes off Cape Breton only to have the boy unable to later save the animal from death.

And as winter defines Canada, so it can be said that hockey characterizes Canadians. Included in this anthology are musings about the curious attachment us northerners can develop for our favourite game. Monica Graham's story of a fight for equal opportunity in sports is enthralling, and David Abbass has delivered a terrific memoir of the joys of building a backyard rink, and youthful imagination fuelling notions of playing in the big leagues. From Norma Jean MacPhee comes a story about the thrill of hometown hockey one cold February night in Cape Breton—the kind of exciting hockey played in rinks throughout Canada each winter. A writer with Miramichi roots, Tom Pond, has composed a special boyhood memoir of the awe-inspiring power and spellbinding magic of a raging ice-jammed river breaking up in early spring. Veteran storyteller Wayne Curtis has crafted a narrative around another mysterious river, a place where, each year, the seasonal rhythms of fishing give way to the frozen pleasures of skating and hockey.

To many Canadians, winter just isn't winter without Christmas. Three stories—by Michael Nowlan, Greta Gaskin Bidlake, and Charlotte and Dan Ross—offer some of the best holiday storytelling from days gone by. Many of our most enduring Christmas memories are heartwarming and inspiring but can also be sad or bittersweet. These festive compilations offer both touching and nostalgic glimpses into what people treasured the most decades ago at Christmastime.

Gary Saunders offers a captivating account of the unique wonders of natural ice found in just about any iced-up brook or pond. And from celebrated Maritime writer Alden Nowlan comes the retelling of a charming Mi'kmaw legend about a man who loathed winter. This Indigenous story is one of my winter favourites; it captures the harshness of nature along with humanity's ability to somehow cope with the elements. Another legend—to contrast Alden Nowlan's narrative—comes from storyteller Steve Vernon. In this charming folk tale, he describes a young boy in Lunenburg who loved winter so much he travelled to the far north in search of Old Man Winter himself.

And from the most easternmost edge of the continent, where extreme winter weather is the rule rather than the exception, come three special stories. These historic narratives are chronicled with astonishing detail and showcase the bravery of stalwart Newfoundlanders facing harsh elements as everyday affairs. And from Labrador comes Harry Paddon's seminal account of the challenging life of yesterday in Canada's frozen north, where travelling by dog team was commonplace.

Each story is encased in a chilly backdrop and each narrative contributes to our appreciation of that strange yet special Canadian characteristic: living in a petrified environment for up to six months each year.

Enjoy!

—*Dan Soucoup*

THE SKATE
Jim Lutes

"No action should be undertaken without aim or other than in conformity with a principle affirming the art of life." —Marcus Aurelius

It is on a piercing cold winter evening, gathered around a fire in the comfortable surroundings of my Rothesay home that I reflect on my notes from an ill-fated adventure I referred to as "The Skate."

My friend and cohort, Allan, has at long last requested my account of this adventure be made public. Heretofore he had asked that the account be suppressed so the lore of the event could grow under its own retelling to become an epic fable, told and retold amongst the society of adventurers to which Allan is a founding member—and the author a reluctant part time participant.

The adventure in question started innocently: a simple phone call suggesting a skate across Nova Scotia. Knowing Allan was never at a loss to exaggerate his endeavours or achievements, I reacted with scepticism. Being otherwise unoccupied by my work as an accountant on this ill-fated day, I chose to respond and listen to the plan in person. I gathered my hockey stick, a windbreaker I use mainly for summer golf, and my fraternity hockey sweater. Given the sunny conditions I did not bring a hat or any other warm clothing. Intending to return by early evening, I left a short note for my wife:

Gone skating with Allan, see you for dinner.
Love Jim

I had recently married and my wife appreciated being advised of my whereabouts. It was a small thing with which I attempted to comply. My occasional transgressions and sometimes-reckless behaviour while away I felt were justified by my habit of this basic courtesy.

Little did I know as I placed the note on the small kitchen table how false and misleading it was to become.

As I steered my '75 Ford Pinto toward the agreed rendezvous point in Waverley, I could have sensed subtle changes in the atmosphere; maybe some sure sign that my life, my long-term mental health, and all my risk-adverse instincts as an accountant were soon to be sorely tested.

My notes suggest I arrived in Waverley at 12:15 P.M. on Saturday, February 21, 1981. As I expected, there was no party to greet me at the door of Allan's home. Quick reconnaissance determined there was a group in the distance, playing hockey on the lake behind the house. The day was clear and the sun sparkled off the clear frozen surface.

I went down to the dock, laced on my skates, and started out toward the crowd.

Being a basketball player and spending time in the gym during winter months had its advantages—being on skates felt liberating and effortless. I would imagine myself as a Jean Ratelle figure, the first-line centre of the New York Rangers. He was the smoothest NHL skater of the time. I could see a plan to finesse my way through a short hockey game, enjoy a beer and rant with Allan and his loose band, then a return home for a pleasant evening with my wife.

The hockey in process was frantic; up and down the ice with two boots on each end marking goals. No one acknowledged me until there was a stoppage in play. Allan skated over. He has a fierce terrier-style aggression. He skated up and stopped just inches in front of me. Even though he is small in stature you sense a maniacal energy that pulses through his frame.

He called the boys over and I realized the only combatants were his two long-time cohorts: Eric, a Stan Rogers tribute artist who also spent time as a pharmacist; and Jack, an Olympic-quality swimmer, as wide and strong as a professional athlete. It was difficult not to observe that neither Eric nor Jack could really skate at all. Jack's stride was more of a clumsy step and both his ankles were turned in. If he were your child, you would have suggested he stick with swimming. Eric was large also, but lankier and had an A&W-rootbeer-bear gut.

I knew both men from other social encounters and had heard their rants at Allan on failed planning and near disasters during canoe or biking adventures. Given their obvious lack of coordination on skates, I felt the accountant had both a style and skill advantage.

After the usual mindless banter and greetings, Allan called the meeting to order. We skated over to his deck that bordered Waverley Lake and sat down to hear the half-baked plan for the day.

Allan produced a map and pointed along the length of Panuke Lake. His theory: this lake, with one portage to a second lake known as Dauphinees Mill Lake, would allow the four of us to cover the width of the province of Nova Scotia. Albeit at its narrowest point. With a skate of a mere forty kilometres, we could lay claim to skating across the province of Nova Scotia.

I mumbled to Al that it didn't seem Eric or Jack knew how to skate; did he really think this made any sense? He was dismissive.

"They'll be fine. These guys have been through a lot more than this. If you don't think Jack can make it, you tell him."

The map was studied by all the erstwhile adventure team. I confess I have no knowledge of topographical maps or directions. I made no contribution but the conversation between the boys got quite heated. Whenever the soundness of judgement of Allan was questioned it was always supported by some large-scale catastrophe the others had experienced at Allan's hands. The examples were not superficial taunts; they seemed fact-based and credible. Over the next thirty minutes a series of near-disastrous outings were relived and all were completely without trust or confidence that Allan had thought it through this time.

I had heard enough to conclude that I would head back to town and leave the boys to their hockey.

As I started to unlace my skates, Allan skated up inches in front of my face again.

"Where are you going? You can't leave me with these two. You will miss a world-class achievement. No one has ever figured this out. It has never been done. The plan is simple, there is a westerly wind. Open your jacket, the wind will push us along. I know Jack and Eric can't skate, but look at them: they can stand up and open their jackets. Jim, you can't disrespect them so much."

I stopped unlacing my skates.

"Ok Al, give me the plan. Now, no bullshit."

The map came out again. "We will be borne by the wind like kites along the thirty kilometres of Panuke Lake. It will take two hours. Then we will make the small traverse and skate the last ten kilometres across Mill Lake. Jack's van is parked at the other end. We'll be back in Waverley by six o'clock. You can be home for dinner by six-thirty. Guaranteed."

I checked my watch. It was 1:45. If the tour was live, we had to leave now.

"Okay Al. You are insane but I need a break from the books and I'm here now—bring it on!"

I laced my skates and headed toward Eric.

Eric is a big affable guy with a genuine smile who is a friend to everyone who knows him. He smiled and winked that we would have to follow the madman on another of his exploits. I asked how he saw the whole thing.

His answer: "As long as the wind cooperates, we are good to go. We are all big enough that the wind will push us along. Al checked and we should have good weather."

The starting point for this marathon was Windsor, Panuke Lake's north end is closest to the town. The ending point was Hubbards on the other side of the province.

We took off our skates and jumped in Allan's van. I was reassured that Jack's van waited at the other end.

The drive was quiet. Even Al was focussed on the road—no radio. No more rants. Even with the wind, forty kilometres was a long skate for a pharmacist, a swimmer, and an accountant. Al was small, fit, and wiry. Even any carnivorous animals we might meet would leave Al alone. I was mentally calculating—I figured a wolf would go for Eric first, Jack second, and me just before Al. I also calculated I was quicker on skates and could sprint ahead of Jack and Eric in order to save myself.

Then it occurred to me: what about ice conditions and the chance of falling through? How did Al know the lake would have solid ice on it? How could he possibly know this? I put the question and Al had an immediate response.

"That's why we carry hockey sticks; hold it sideways and it'll keep your head above water if you break through."

It was too late to turn back now since we had driven the forty minutes to Windsor, but my spider sense tingled. This was going to be a long afternoon.

We jumped out of the van and climbed down the hill to put on our skates at the edge of the lake.

Al told us to tie the laces of our boots together and hang them around our necks.

"Okay Al, but why? Aren't we skating?" I asked.

"Yes, but you will need boots for the traverse," he replied. "We have to leave the ice and hike to the second lake."

I look out the side of my eye at Allan. He was smiling. It seemed he had a plan but we were still in early days.

The first few strides were exhilarating. The ice was glass. The sun was reflecting off the surface and there was a faint feeling of spring warmth.

Al went immediately to the centre of the lake alone. I stayed with Eric and Jack, and, as we got moving, they both had better form than I expected. Neither would make the NHL but both were efficient and moving forward.

I suddenly felt a huge release. I had been buried in chartered accountant exam preparations for months and had not breathed enough clean air. The relentless pressure of the upcoming exams was bearing down on me. The date to write the exams was cast in stone and I could feel each day checked off toward that challenge. My father was a partner in the CA firm I worked for. To succeed on the exams was an essential rite of passage. To fail was inconceivable. I had worked it out of proportion in my own mind and a good long skate would clear the cobwebs and give me fresh perspective.

Almost immediately the boys were grumbling that something was wrong. We were working our way along but there was no helping wind. Any breeze that existed seemed to be right in our faces. It wasn't impossible to overcome a light breeze but it wasn't helping. Forty kilometres of honest skating versus "kite" skating were two very different things.

Allan had set off ahead. He was exactly in the centre of the lake and the three of us were following the shore.

"I wonder if it's safe out there for him on his own. Shouldn't one of us go out there with him?" Eric mused to no one specific.

Neither Jack nor I made a move and kept skating forward. In my mind, if Eric wanted to skate with Allan he could fill his boots. I was staying by the shore with Jack.

The wind started to gain strength. It was like someone had hold of your jacket and was pulling on it from behind. We three had fallen into a pattern: one guy in the lead and the other two close behind. We were applying the principals of drafting to skating. Take your turn in the front and then drop back. Both Eric and Jack were wide guys. From behind one or both of them you were in a mini air pocket. It seemed warmer and less windy. It was almost like being dragged along. At the front it was getting worse with each rotation. My golf jacket, all the cover I had, was flapping hard and inflating around my arms and back. I tried to tighten the zipper at the neck to prevent air from entering, but the jacket always returned to being a balloon.

We were making steady progress but not at speed, and it was all work.

Eric and Jack had started to malign Al for his lack of plan and the windy conditions. It must be going to change. Forty kilometres directly into a headwind was not possible.

Jack admitted he had hardly been on skates since high school. He was about thirty-five, so that meant no practice in twenty years. His skates looked like heirlooms, old-school blades and discoloured laces.

But the peloton took shape. Jack, Eric, then me. Jack drops back, Eric in front, me in the middle. Then Eric back, me in front, and Jack right behind. We were into an even rotation, each man with a sense of pride to take his turn at the front. The protocol became stay there until the guy behind gives you a tap—he is saying he is ready to go, good work—yet maybe he is watching to see if you are losing steam.

Lost in our routine, we three didn't notice when Al appeared at our side. The solo adventurer from the middle of the lake had come for a checkpoint. He skated in front and signalled us to come to shore. We veered off to follow him. Behind a big rock and out of the wind, Al produced the map. The boys studied it for a matter of moments and all agreed: five kilometres down. We had been skating for forty-five minutes. Slow progress. At this rate we were in for a seven- to eight-hour skate. Time for a vote: turn back and try another day when the wind was better, or keep on?

Al was belligerent. He immediately launched into a poorly thought out rant: "We can't even think about turning back. If you guys maintained any level of fitness we would be halfway there. This wind will change. If you guys want to turn back, give me your keys. I am going to finish this alone."

Al was so fired up he didn't notice that no one was paying attention. Eric was having a piss, Jack was laying back on a rock, and I was half listening out of a sense of duty. Al usually stops yelling faster if he thinks someone is listening.

Eric told me he was sure the wind would change soon. He assured me he would never rely on Allan for anything as critical as weather—

he had checked himself and the wind direction was forecasted to change.

Immediately on starting back on the rotation, the wind strength was up. I couldn't tell if I was tired and imagining it or if it was real. It felt like the front end of a gale. The wind was directly in my face, so hard I could feel my skin reacting.

Within a half hour snow started. The ice was still clear but light snow was now whipping back at us. It was not my imagination; the wind was gale force.

My memory is cloudy for the next four or five hours. It seemed endless. All I remember is Eric's ass. When I was not in front I got my nose as close to his ass as I could to take the cover and protection. I worked hard to stay close and I feared I would fall back and they would leave me.

I went to the front when Eric had to drop. I watched him closely. I didn't want to burn him out so each turn seemed to be shorter and shorter for both Eric and I as we struggled against the blow. Jack kept extending his role in front. He would not give in. He seemed to be gaining strength as the evening wore on.

Everything seemed to be dark and desolate, and even though the boys were close I felt alone. I have a very strong will and I was not going to slow them down or give up. I calculated my time in front by strides. I tried to make every one count. The monotony was grinding. No thoughts, just survival. The snow had slowed down but it was still piercing cold. I felt I had to keep moving to stay warm.

In the distance Al was barely visible. He seemed solid but I wondered how long it could be before he came in. Jack decided we needed a rest. He took us toward the shore where there were rocks for protection. I huddled behind a large boulder and immediately went to sleep. Never had a rock felt so warm and welcoming. In what seemed like a minute Eric was shaking me awake.

"We have to go." Then, like he was just noticing for the first time: "Why are you wearing a golf jacket? It's winter. Have you got enough clothes on? Didn't Al tell you we'd be out overnight?"

I shook off the comment thinking we must be close to the end of the lake. I could see Jack slowing down. He had iron will but he was almost walking now. The wind was fierce in our faces and every stride was a battle, whether I was behind Eric or out in front. My back and knees were cramping—too much time bent over and working. Each time I had to go in front I pushed harder. Share the load and keep the pace.

Just when it felt like we would die out there on the ice, a narrow point at the end of the lake came into view. It was in the distance but I could see it. Each time in front it got closer.

We were almost there. Short walk in the woods, short skate, drive home...hope.

We reached the shore and sat together. Brutal night but two smiles. Both Eric and Jack had second wind and could feel the end. I caught the vibe and smiled back. No conversation.

We laced up our boots and started over dry land for the woods. Part way up the hill we all turned around.

Where the hell was Allan?

Before the thought was fully formed he came bounding out of the woods at the top of the hill waving both arms.

"This way boys, short walk ahead."

Eric glanced at Jack and asked the obvious. "Shouldn't we look at the map and confirm our location? Al can't be trusted. We've been here before. No time now for a mistake."

But Al had already turned and was stomping over the hill. Too late to question or stop. We had to start right away to keep him in sight. He seemed sure of himself and was moving quickly.

We fell into the same pattern: Jack in front, then Eric, then me. Jack never let up. He was like a bull through the snow. Seemed like he was pissed off and just wanted to be done.

Eric confirmed that, based on what he remembered, the walk through the woods should only be about ten minutes. Then we'd be back on skates to get to the van.

We pounded forward. Every few minutes one of us would break through the surface crust and end up waist-deep in snow. The others would pause and wait until you wrestled your way back to your feet. The trail Al was following was not straight. He was wandering from side to side like he had lost something. He seemed set on a general direction but I could feel us drifting off line, if we were ever on a line.

After forty minutes it was clear we were lost. I was soaked from the waist down and shivering constantly. There was no sign of the second lake. The moon was up but the darkness had fully closed in. The next step was not clear.

Al had slowed in front, and without special effort we caught up.

I sat down in the snow and lay back while the others talked. Voices quickly became raised. There was a different tone to the conversation. I was far enough away that I could not hear exactly what was being said, but I heard my name a few times.

Finally Eric came over.

"Decision made. We are going to stop, make a fire, and dry out. Al has no idea where we are. We are lost in the woods in central Nova Scotia. No one here knows where we are and no one will come to help. We have to warm up and think this through."

I stumbled around gathering things I thought would burn and brought them to the pile. Before long we had a substantial mound of wood. Jack was separating it and made a base. It caught fire on the first match and before long there was a roaring warm glow.

I got in as close as I could and sat down on a rock. The heat was instant. I could see the steam hissing and rising off my pants.

Off to the side Allan and Jack were having a heated conversation. After some back and forth, I saw Jack force the map from Al's hand and start walking off at a ninety-degree angle from the direction we had been travelling.

He disappeared over the hill. Within minutes was back at the fire.

"I climbed a tree and the lake is right there. But I can determine we have circled it twice following Al. We'll be skating in five minutes boys."

I was reluctant to leave. In an act of kindness rare in our forty-year relationship, Allan came over and asked if I was warm enough. I told him I was frozen but I would make it. He took off his jacket, pulled his vest over his head, and pushed it at me.

"Put this on. It's wool. It will keep your core warm"

I thought for a second about turning him down. Then I thought how he had dragged me out here and how I wouldn't feel bad if he froze. I pulled it over my head and put my jacket on over it before he could change his mind.

Jack had buried the fire in snow and it was time to move. I followed him and ignored Al.

After a short climb we were at the edge of another beautiful clear lake. The moon was now directly overhead, reflecting off the frozen water, making it look like a large glass stage under spotlights.

I was quick to lace on my skates.

Jack pointed the direction and I took off.

I felt the same exhilaration as I did at the start. The ice seemed like it had just been properly flooded by a Zamboni. There was not a crack or a blemish.

With the warmth of the vest and the knowledge that we were close, I turned into Jean Ratelle again. In my mind's eye I was skating perfectly. One thing was for sure: the boys were losing ground. I thought about turning back but I figured they might want private time with Al to ream him out for the near disaster he had planned.

When they arrived at the far shore I had my boots on and was waiting by the van. Any adrenaline I had found on the lake was gone. I was exhausted and couldn't stand without leaning on the van.

Jack had the van started and warmed up quickly and we were on our way. I have no memory of the drive. Eric shook me awake and said to get in with Al, he would take me home.

Al was behind the wheel and we headed for the city. I had an upstairs apartment in North End Halifax, an older industrial area.

We pulled into my driveway at 4:15 A.M. No one had cellphones in those days so I wasn't sure what mood I would face from my wife when I stumbled in.

I trudged up the stairs and opened the front door. She was sitting on the couch by the phone and seemed shocked to see me.

She stood up and came toward me, crying.

"I was worried *sick*. You should have been home twelve hours ago! I've called the hospitals and the police and they would have been searching for you at first light."

She hugged me warmly. "I'm so glad you are safe. Where have you been?"

"Allan is a madman. Keep him away from me. He has no idea what he is doing. We could have died out there."

"Go take a warm bath, you must be frozen."

I did as she suggested. The warm water was a luxury. I settled down and my legs and back started to loosen up.

Just when I was starting to relax I heard Allan's voice in the living room. He was talking and laughing and Colina wasn't saying much.

He poked his head into the bathroom.

"Take care old buddy. We'll catch up soon. You can tell your grandkids about this one." And he was off.

I could have choked him or attempted to drown him but I didn't have the energy. As I settled back down I smiled and knew it would be a great story for the kids and grandkids, whenever either arrived.

Al is still my friend, I see Eric whenever I can, and they tell me Jack lives on a farm. The idea of skating across Nova Scotia at night into a gale-force wind would never cross my mind now. In the forty years since The Skate, whenever I have faced big challenges that needed to be overcome by force of will, I have hunkered down and pushed through, knowing I can. I expect I'll face a few more challenges before I finish the fourth quarter of my life, and I still have The Skate to give me the strength I'll need.

MOON TIDE
Sara Jewell

After a final mop of his plate with a slice of brown bread, John shoves the last bite of his supper into his mouth as he pushes his chair back from the table.

"Wait for me," his older brother Kenny says.

"Take your plates to the sink, boys," their mother says, and they clatter knives and forks and plates onto the counter.

Although they love their mother's pot roast and gravy and boiled potatoes, especially during a mid-winter deep freeze, John and Kenny are eager to get back outside. Normally, coats and hats will do but tonight they know they'll need knitted scarves tied around their necks as well. The boys each pull on an extra pair of Granny's knitted wool socks then jam their feet into their calf-high boots, tying the laces tightly. John flings open the outer door and jumps down the steps, Kenny right behind him.

"Look!" he calls out, his breath appearing in front of him in one quick puff. He points to the sky—the large white moon rising full and round above the frozen river. Their boots crunch as they make their way across the snow-covered yard.

Inside the barn, the air is warm and damp as thirty beef cattle stand in their stanchions waiting for one last feed of grain and water. At eleven and thirteen, John and Kenny are old enough to do the evening chores on their own. The boys are scurrying around the barn, one with a water bucket and the other with a feed scoop, when their father walks in. He grabs a pitchfork and jerks his head at the door.

"Are you sure, Dad?" Kenny asks but John shoves past him.

"All right! Thanks, Dad," John says as he drops the feed scoop back into the grain bin and heads outside. Moving from the warm air of the barn to the crisp cold takes his breath away and he holds a wool mitten to his mouth for a moment. Kenny follows him across the yard.

"Be careful, boys," their father calls after them from the barn. "Remember—it's a moon tide."

The snowmobiles are parked in the old garage next to the original homestead. As they pass by the house where their father grew up, the brothers see Granny sitting near the living room window. They wave, knowing she is sitting in Grandpa's rocking chair over the cast-iron floor grate radiating heat from the furnace up into the house.

"It's not too cold for them to start, is it?" John wonders.

"Let's hope not," Kenny answers. Stepping onto one of the snowmobiles, he twists the key, turns on the choke, and then yanks the pull-cord several times. The snowmobile does not start.

"It's too cold," John says.

"It's just starting hard," Kenny tells him, yanking again. The engine sputters then catches and black smoke puffs out the exhaust pipe, filling the garage with the stench of gas and oil.

John climbs onto the second sled, the one he's nicknamed King of the Road, and starts it easily. As the boys wait for their machines to warm up, John bangs his mittened hands together to generate some heat before they head out into the wind that always blows over the river. With the clear sky and full moon, it will be icy-cold tonight.

Gunning the engines, the boys circle the house once for their mother's sake then race across the field and down the embankment to the shore, where they point their sleds downriver. The river is fed by water draining down from the hills and eventually empties into a bay, which eventually empties into the Northumberland Strait, which eventually empties into the Atlantic Ocean. John imagines the water running by his family's farm in northwestern Nova Scotia could once have been in the ocean. John has never been to the coast, has never put a foot into the Atlantic Ocean, but he believes when he swims in the river, it's almost the same thing. It's almost as if the ocean isn't really so far away.

Even though he is a farm boy, John watches the river constantly, noting throughout the day whether the tide is high or low. Even when he is at school, John thinks about the tide. He loves farming but he loves the river, too—its beauty, its mystery, its routine.

Everything is frozen solid tonight. The third week of January came in with a savage cold; it has been minus-thirty for the past few nights. That keeps the cattle in the barn but also builds up the river ice hard and fast. John knows it's safe to drive on. He also knows that despite the deep freeze—in fact, because of it—the fishers will be out on the ice. With the full moon lighting up the sky, it is the perfect night for fishing smelts on the river.

The snowmobiles fly over a sharp dip in the ice but neither boy notices. If they had, they would have known it means the tide is almost out and lower than usual because of the full moon. The ice has dropped, creating the dip.

John lets out a loud "whoop!" as he grips the handlebars and gives the snowmobile more speed, passing his older, more cautious brother with a wide grin. He loves the thrill of driving at night over the frozen water; it stretches out before him, a shimmering silver ribbon. The cold air bites his skin and makes his eyes water, but he finds it exhilarating, not painful.

When the two machines round the long curve in front of the Henley farm, lights twinkle in the distance—the gas lanterns of the smelt fishers. The lanterns are hanging from tall poles called "pickets" that are driven down through a hole in the ice into the bottom of the river. Every fisher has to buy a licence to fish in one particular spot, and that spot is called a "set." The sets are spread out to give each fisher ample space.

To John, the lights stretching along the ice look like a village. John slows down, allowing Kenny to catch up. Driving side by side now, the boys wave as they buzz past fishers hauling their full bag nets up through the ice. When they reach Old Ray's set, they pull alongside. At either end of a long, narrow cut in the ice, two pickets holding Old Ray's bag net are staked through the ice deep into the mud on the bottom of the river. A long pole called a "braile" stretches between the two pickets. Like all the other sets, gas lanterns light up the hole in the ice.

Old Ray is standing next to a half a dozen crates filled with small, silvery smelts. Another dozen crates are stacked on shore next to his fishing shanty. He waves the boys in, his face almost hidden by his white beard and the green woollen cap he has pulled down to cover his ears.

"Great night for fishing," Kenny says as he dismounts his snowmobile and walks over to the older man. "Dad says a moon tide really brings the fish in."

"You just missed the chance to help me bring up my net, boys," Old Ray grumbles good-naturedly. "I could have put you to work filling those crates."

"We could help with the next haul, sir," Kenny says.

Old Ray cuffs Kenny's wool hat. "That's another six hours, son. The tide is coming back in now and we fish the tides, you know. The current brings the fish into the net, which is shaped like a bag. But the net has to be turned around in order to fish the tide when it changes."

"What happens if you forget to turn the net around?" John asks.

Old Ray lets loose a bark of laughter. "Then your net turns inside out and you lose all your smelts. Here, to take home with you. Your mother will cook these up for breakfast."

Grabbing a small plastic bucket, Old Ray reaches into one of the crates and scoops up a bucketful of smelts. He snaps on a lid and hands it to Kenny.

"They don't get any fresher than that."

"Thank you, Mr. Henley," Kenny says.

John blows his warm breath through his mittens.

"You boys want something warm to drink?" Old Ray says. "C'mon, I'll put water on to boil."

Kenny places the bucket on the ice next to his snowmobile and he and John follow Old Ray across the ice and into his onshore shanty. All the fishers have them; it's how they stay warm for the four or five days they live on the ice while the smelts are running. Old Ray's shanty is about the size of John's bedroom but made from planks of rough wood, not plastered, and definitely not insulated.

There is a wooden table with three wooden chairs inside, next to an old bunk covered in a dark grey wool blanket. The boys sit in the chairs as Old Ray stokes up the wood stove and repositions a kettle to the middle of the stove, where the already-warm water will quickly come to a boil. Against one wall is a set of coarse shelves where Old Ray keeps a few plates and mugs, a loaf of homemade bread, a jar of jam, a tin of tea bags, and a hunk of cheese wrapped in cloth. He grabs two mugs and puts them on the table next to his own, which he picks up and tosses the dregs into one corner of the shanty. He drops a fresh tea bag into each of the mugs.

When the kettle comes to a boil, he fills each mug with hot water then fetches a jar of milk from where it sits on the ice against one wall. A tin of sugar is already on the table, next to a spoon.

He nods at the boys to help themselves. John pours in enough milk to cool the tea along with two scoops of sugar.

Kenny glares at him. "Don't be a pig," he hisses.

"That's all right, boy, you take as much as you need," Old Ray says. "It's a cold night to be on the river."

Old Ray stirs a spoonful of sugar into his tea, takes a sip, and then scowls at the heat.

"How are your parents?" he asks.

"They're fine, Mr. Henley," Kenny says. "Mother made roast for supper tonight and Dad let us out of chores so we could go for a ride."

"Have any of the cows started to calf yet?"

"No, sir, not yet, but soon, I expect. A couple are close. Dad hopes they'll wait until this deep freeze breaks."

Old Ray nods at John. "You snaring rabbits this winter, young man?"

John swallows his mouthful of tea and nods. "Yes, sir. I've sold a dozen to the general store in Port Howe."

"Good for you. That's good, honest work."

"What will you do with all your smelts, Mr. Henley?" Kenny asks.

"Same as your brother does with his rabbits." He takes another gulp of tea. "I'll sell what I can to our neighbours, and the rest I'll sell to the fish buyer down at the end of the river."

Old Ray tips his mug back and finishes his tea. "Boys, I hate to break up this party but I have to mend the net before it goes back in the water." He stands up. "Just leave your mugs there, I'll clean up later."

"Thanks for the tea," John says.

"Yes, and thank you for the smelts, Mr. Henley," Kenny says as he and John return to their snowmobiles.

Kenny puts the bucket of smelts on the seat between his legs.

"You're welcome. Tell your parents I'll be along for a visit once the smelt stop running. And you boys be careful heading back up the river. Don't go too fast."

Driving slowly, the boys weave their way through the village of sets, the twinkling gas lanterns casting golden shadows that dance on the ice. When the last set is behind them, the boys head toward home, the full moon transforming the frozen river into a gleaming trail.

"Don't go too fast, little brother," Kenny warns as John gives his machine more gas.

"There's nothing to worry about," John calls back, the wind snatching his words out of his mouth.

The snowmobiles speed along, the cold bringing tears to the brothers' eyes and pulling their bright blue scarves straight out behind them.

As they round the final bend before the farm and see the yard light by the barn shining in the darkness, John guns the engine and pulls out ahead of his older brother with a happy holler.

"Last one home is a rotten egg!"

"Hey, no fair!" Kenny yells, revving his engine, clenching the bucket of smelts tighter between his legs.

John is still laughing when suddenly the nose of his snowmobile dips. He hears a splash and his sled jerks to a stop. He cuts the engine then stands on his running boards to get a better look. His skis are wedged under a lip of ice, while a thin layer of water has pooled on top of the ice that has broken off.

"What's wrong?" Kenny calls.

Their father has explained that with a full moon come extreme tides. When the tide is very low, the ice over the shallow water along the shoreline can drop enough to touch the bottom of the river. If the ice is sticking to the bottom when the tide comes back in, the ice doesn't rise and water floods in on top of it.

But there is no danger; the water isn't deep enough to flood John's engine.

"Hey!" John calls out to his brother as he hops off his sled. "The ice stuck to the bottom here. Come here, help pull me out."

Kenny hops off his snowmobile and goes for the toolbox on the back of his brother's sled. Along with spare spark plugs, a spark plug wrench, a screwdriver, and a spare drive belt, the boys both carry a strong rope with them for emergencies just like this. Kenny ties the rope to the bar at the back of John's snowmobile and together, the boys pull it out of the shallow puddle.

"Maybe our next snowmobiles will have a reverse gear on them," John says, panting.

"You wouldn't need one if you'd slow down and keep an eye out."

John punches his brother in the arm then hops on his sled and turns it on. Kenny pulls alongside his brother and they sit astride their snowmobiles, engines throttling quietly, gazing at the bright moon in the sky and the frozen river around them, their breath puffing into the air.

"C'mon, let's head into town," John says. "It's so bright out and we can be there in fifteen minutes."

"But Dad—"

John cuts him off. "Dad won't mind," he says. "Chores are done and we have enough gas. What could happen? We know the way and the river is frozen solid."

John revs his engine and drives off, continuing upriver. Kenny catches up and the boys travel side by side, passing a couple more sets with their twinkling gas lanterns. They give a big wave to Mr. Mitchell at the curve in the river, the last good fishing spot before the water becomes shallower. It will open up again near town and the boys think about reaching the ball field where they can drive ashore and follow the trails through town, maybe meet up with some of their friends.

As the river narrows, John pulls ahead of his brother and speeds up. He loves to drive fast and there might not be another chance this winter to be on the river under a full moon in a clear sky.

"I'm King of the River!" John hollers as he stands up and waves an arm in the air.

The snowmobile hits a bump and bounces, slamming John back. There is a splash and a gurgle: the machine lands in open water. The moon's reflection ripples over black.

The front end of John's sled has disappeared into deep, slushy water the colour of ink.

Without turning, John senses that part of the track has hooked on the rough ice at the edge of the water and is holding the snowmobile— and him—in a safe but precarious position.

"John, what happened?" Kenny calls from behind, alarmed by the angle of his brother's snowmobile. John cuts his engine. Kenny pulls up behind him.

"I hit water, Kenny, and it's deep," John says. He turns to look at his brother and the snowmobile slips, its nose sliding further into the water.

"Don't move!" Kenny cries. "Stay still." He looks around and sees a small cabin behind the trees lining the shore. "We're at Charlie's lot," he tells his brother. "It's that shallow spot where the reefs get us every summer in the boat."

"So the ice must have dropped in the tide and stuck to the bottom."

"But that never happens in the middle of the river," Kenny says.

"Then what happened?"

"Doesn't matter. I gotta pull you out."

John looks uncertain. "Can you do it by yourself? What if I fall off?"

The boys stare at each other.

"Don't move, Johnny. I'm going back to get Dad. We need his help."

"No! Don't leave me, Kenny," John cries, but Kenny is already running to his snowmobile. He fires it up and tears away back downriver.

Very soon, the sound of his brother's snowmobile fades. Alone in the moonlight, John is enveloped by silence.

Only a frozen river is anything but silent: creaks and groans, gurgles and splashes start to fill the air. The ice snaps as it rises with the tide. Will the water get higher? Did his snowmobile just move?

Suddenly, the ice beneath him gives a great *craaack*! Panic rises in John's chest.

Stay calm, he tells himself. *Dad and Kenny will be back soon.*

John hears his father's voice in his head, warning of the dangers of falling through ice in wintertime: "You'll freeze so quick, you won't be able to tread water or pull yourself out, son," his father has said over and over. "Summer or winter, you don't fool around with the water."

John has no idea how secure his snowmobile is on the edge of the ice; any sudden movement might be enough to shift it loose and slide the machine—and him—into the deep, black, frigid water.

John is sure he feels cold water seeping into his boots. In the distance, an owl hoots. This is the first time he has been alone on the river in the dark. The moon is like a spotlight in the sky shining down on him, stranded by a huge hole in the ice. The ice cracks again and water begins to lap over the running boards.

John hears a sound and almost turns his body towards it before he remembers not to move.

The drone of a snowmobile engine gets louder and John sees a light bouncing across the ice. It's either his father and Kenny, or someone else out for an evening ride. John hopes it is his father.

The light pulls up nearby. The engine cuts out and the light shuts off.

"John! I'm here, son," his father calls out.

As John turns to look, his father shouts, "No! Don't move, John."

John freezes. It's hard to stay still. He is cold now that his feet are wet.

"I have two ropes," his father tells him. "I'm going to tie one to the bar on the back of your sled, then toss the second to you to tie around your waist. Kenny will hold onto that one to keep you on your seat when I pull it back. Okay, son? You okay?"

"I'm okay, Dad," John manages to answer. The cold has seeped into his clothes and he's beginning to shiver. "I'm a little c-cold, that's all."

"We'll have you inside by the fire in no time," his dad reassures him. His voice is close behind as he ties a rope to the back of the snowmobile. He nudges John's elbow and says, "Here's the rope. I'm going to toss it over your head so it lands on your lap. Don't grab it until it is close enough that you don't have to lean forward. Okay?"

"Okay, Dad."

The first toss glances off the right handlebar and falls into the water, making a quiet splash. The second toss falls across his left knee and John tries to reach it but as he leans forward, the snowmobile wobbles.

"John, stop!"

The rope drops into the water. John slowly sits back.

"Try again, D-Dad."

Moon Tide

His teeth are chattering. The third throw lands across his thighs and John grabs the rope with both hands, his grip slow and stiff from the cold in his fingers.

"John, I want you to tie the rope around your waist but move *very slowly*," his father says.

John positions the rope around his waist and yanks off his mittens to make two strong knots. But his fingers are so cold they fumble the rope. It slips through his right hand.

"Oh, no!" John cries but just in time, his left hand pins the rope to his leg.

"What happened?" Kenny asks.

"My h-hands are too…too c-cold to t-tie the knots."

"Hold the rope under your armpit and blow into your hands," his father tells him. "You've got to get that rope tied around you."

John does as his father tells him and is able to warm his fingers up enough to work the rope. It occurs to him that it would be even better to wrap the rope around twice before tying the knots.

"Good thinking, boy," his father says. "Let me know when you're ready."

"I'm r-ready, Dad," John says and squeezes his eyes shut.

"All right, son, I'm going to use the other snowmobile to pull yours out of the water and Kenny will hang onto the rope attached to you. When you feel the snowmobile move, you grab the handlebars and hang on for dear life, okay?"

His father's footsteps crunch away. The other snowmobile fires up and the engine revs.

"Ready, John?" Kenny calls out.

"R-ready," John answers, his lips too cold to move.

He feels the rope attached to his sled tighten. The snowmobile beneath him begins to sway side to side. John pitches forward, grabbing the handlebars as the snowmobile jerks backwards. Water rushes out from under the hood back into the river. The rope around John's waist tightens as Kenny takes up the slack. His father guns his snowmobile again and the one underneath John lurches to one side as its back end jerks onto the ice.

John's hands are too cold to hold onto the handlebars and as his grip loosens, there is a roar from his father's sled as he accelerates. John's snowmobile is yanked up onto the surface of the ice. And John tumbles into the water.

"John!" Kenny screams.

Thick, freezing water hits John in the face. He chokes. His body stiffens as he flounders, trying to get his bearings; his feet not touching bottom, his bare hands not touching ice. He is too cold to move and the water is pressing in on him. His clothes are soaked through and heavy. He feels his wet coat dragging him further under.

The rope around his waist squeezes and he is pulled through the slushy water.

"We've got you, son," his father grunts, lying on his stomach on the ice with his chest resting against the bump that sent John's sled into the trough. Both his arms reach out over the edge towards John.

"Keeping pulling, Kenny! Bring him in."

Water splashes into John's eyes as he tries to reach for his father's hand. Kenny pulls him close enough for his father to grab the rope, then John's coat, then John himself, pulling the boy over the lip of ice and to safety.

John's father scrambles to his knees and scoops John into his arms. John can't feel the rough material of his father's coat against his frozen cheeks.

"D-d-d-daaa—" John tries to speak. His entire body is shivering uncontrollably.

"Kenny, I'm taking John home. See if you can start his sled. I'll come back for you."

John's father throws a leg over the seat of his still-running snowmobile and puts John down in front of him. With one arm wrapped tightly around his youngest son, he punches the throttle and tears off in the direction of the farm.

"We'll have you home and in front of the stove in no time, son," he says, his warm lips against John's frozen ear.

The cold night air whips against John's skin as the snowmobile races along the ice, but John's father doesn't slow down until he reaches the back steps of the house. Through his watering eyes, John sees his mother standing at the door, her hands pressed against her mouth.

"Get a blanket, Isabelle," his father instructs. "John fell in."

John's father follows her as she rushes back into the house and grabs the wool blanket draped over the back of the old couch. Once inside the warm room, his father lowers John to the floor.

"Stand up, John, we have to get you out of these clothes."

John stands, swaying, as his father strips the wet clothes off him—coat, shirt, undershirt, long johns, socks—and his mother wraps the scratchy but warm blanket around him. His father helps him take the few steps towards his chair next to the wood stove. The heat stings John's frozen body.

John's mother brings her son a steaming mug half full of hot water. She wraps John's shaking fingers around it, keeping her hands over his, helping him hold it steady. Eventually, he lifts it to his mouth and takes a sip.

"H-h-hot," John says.

John's father looks down at him and seems relieved. "Your lips aren't blue anymore. You okay?"

John nods.

They hear a snowmobile pull up outside. The engine cuts off then footsteps pound up the back steps.

"That'll be Kenny. Guess he was able to get your sled started," John's father says.

"Drink your hot water, John, while I make you boys some hot chocolate," his mother says, placing a hand on his shoulder and kissing his half-dry hair.

Kenny bursts into the kitchen calling, "Is he all right?" He sees John in their father's chair by the stove, wrapped in a blanket, holding a mug.

"He'll be fine," his father answers.

"John, man, that was close," Kenny says, his voice quavering.

"Look. Got these out of the water." He holds up John's mittens, frozen stiff. "I'll hang 'em by the fire."

John gradually stops shivering as he warms up. He gets hot enough that he has to shove the blanket off his shoulders when the hot chocolate arrives. Steam rises from his mittens as they dry. His parents sit around the kitchen table drinking tea while Kenny sprawls on the couch drinking his hot chocolate.

Tonight, their mother added marshmallows, a treat usually reserved for special occasions.

"Dad, what happened out there? Could the ice really have dropped to the bottom of the river?" Kenny asks.

"Remember that thaw we had at the beginning of January?" he asks Kenny and looks over at John, too. "I was lying on hunks of ice when I was grabbing for John so that makes me think that part of the river must have broken up during that thaw. That made the ice stack up on those reefs you boys always manage to get the row boat stuck on during low tide in the summer. So when the ice froze again, that left an open spot at the edge of those stacks of ice. Even in this cold, that would be open water because of the tide," he adds. "Every time the tide came in, that spot filled up and it's extra deep tonight because of the moon tide. If you were going fast and not paying attention, you'd hit that spot without any warning."

John's father turns and fixes his younger son with a serious stare.

"I warned you boys about the moon tide," he says sternly. "You can't be reckless on the water, boy, not in winter or summer. You have to keep watching all the time. That cold water, boy, it could've killed you." He takes a sip of his tea. "How fast were you going, John?"

If his father knew he was hollering "I'm King of the River" when he hit that bump in the ice and slid into the water, John knows he'd never be allowed on the snowmobile again. John glances at Kenny who lifts his mug to his mouth, hiding the tiny shake of his head.

"I'll be more careful in the future. You can bet on it," John answers his father, grateful his brother won't tell on him. "I've learned my lesson."

His father stares hard at him, opens his mouth, and then sits back with a nod. "I don't doubt that. All right, we'll leave it at that."

"Thanks, Dad. And thanks, Kenny," John adds. He suddenly remembers what his brother was carrying when they left the sets downriver. "Hey, Kenny, whatever happened to the smelts Old Ray gave us? We didn't lose them, did we?"

His brother looks up from his mug of hot chocolate. "Oh, no. I brought them in when I came to get Dad."

Their father laughs and ruffles Kenny's hair. "He saved both you and the smelts."

John smiles. "I'm sure going to enjoy eating those for breakfast tomorrow."

"A breakfast fit for a king, right, brother?" Kenny says with a wink.

SKIING ACROSS THE HIGHLANDS:
A WILDERNESS ADVENTURE
Scott Cunningham

*T*he silence hung heavier than the snow-laden boughs. It sensitized us to those few sounds we had brought with us into this remote area: the rhythmic squeaking under the skis, the crackling of nylon jackets and gators, and our laboured breathing as we inched onwards with our fifty-pound packs weighing on our shoulders. Our ears had become amplifiers, catching those minor movements that would be lost in the background activity of town and country.

Then, an abrupt snap. I froze. My confused senses attempted to evaluate the chaos of breaking branches. But before I could adjust, a huge bull moose disappeared into the thicket. The silence resettled, broken only by the squeaking of the snow, our laboured breath.

For most, the Cape Breton Highlands National Park means the Cabot Trail with its panoramic ocean vistas and brilliant autumn colours. These are found on the coastal fringes of the park and are what most visitors see and appreciate. But another area, in fact the bulk of this park, separates Cheticamp from Ingonish and is inaccessible except for a few primitive trails.

It is both the highest and oldest region of Nova Scotia—an inhospitable area. In the summer heat, bugs infest the bogs and barrens where the patchy forest has seen better days. In winter the snow arrives early and departs late. Temperatures drop well below the freezing point and the winds, which sweep in across the Gulf ice, cut through the gorges and over the plateaus churning up a frenzy of snow that can equal any Arctic storm. Travellers are few.

Of course, this remoteness does have it attractions. The botanist will discover Arctic-alpine flora, a carry-over from the last glaciation when the plateau was an oasis in a sea of ice. It is also the last bastion of the lynx and the only nesting area in the province for the greater yellowlegs. But it is for the moose that these highlands are particularly noted. These large mammals are common, relatively safe from humans and brainworm, a debilitating and lethal parasite that has reduced its numbers in the rest of the province.

Crossing this park is not an everyday occurrence; I have only attempted it twice. The first time was years ago when I hiked up the Cheticamp River gorge. Unfortunately, the cliff and waterfalls slowed my pace and a knee infection forced my retreat onto one of the pulp roads that join the park boundary. Recently, I decided to try again. To avoid heat and bugs, as well as cliffs, the plan was to go over the top—during winter.

Fortunately, I had been able to convince Dave Lawry of Parks Canada that I possessed the equipment and knowledge required to cross the highlands. He gave us tips on the terrain and the trails (or lack thereof) and drove us to the departure point on top of French Mountain.

The first two days were idyllic. Fair weather clouds skimmed overhead, almost within reach. The temperature was only slightly below zero and a light covering of powder snow, over a four-to-five-foot base was ideal for cross-country skiing.

In the second evening a full moon, hanging in the clear frozen sky, invited us out of the tent onto the undulating carpet of a sparsely treed plateau. No roads, fences, or no-trespassing signs hindered our freedom to descend and climb, turn or stop, where and when we pleased. No cars or snowmobiles or chain saws. And no wind. Just a blanket of white, reflecting the moonlight with the brilliance of crystal. Occasionally the piercing crack of a splitting tree trunk shattered the peace.

We explored the upper reaches of the MacKenzie River where it was little more than a stream hidden under ice and snow, now and then coming up for air. Moose tracks and scat were as common here as along the rabbit trails near my home on the Eastern Shore. Here we encountered another of these enormous animals, this time with her calf, quietly feeding on nutritious twigs and buds along the scarcely discernible riverbank. They paid us little heed.

Gradually we adjusted to the realities of winter camping. Although blackflies and mosquitoes are not a problem, almost everything else can be. Temperatures are, of course, lower this time of year but even more important are the extreme fluctuations common in our Maritime climate. Snow may fall, but so may rain—or sleet or hail. Keeping dry and warm is a major chore, and a fundamental concern, for that insidious specter, hypothermia, can rapidly creep up upon the unwary. You need to eat and drink more than usual and set up camp early in the afternoon.

In deep snow, lounging around an evening campfire is out of the question. If it doesn't sink out of sight from its own heat, your front will steam while your back will freeze. Don't plan on dismounting from your skis before the site has been well compacted or you may suddenly find yourself up to your waist and immobile. Ski touring also means dealing with stiff boots, frozen water bottles, and clumsily manipulating everything with either mittened hands or numb fingers. And, of course, there is that matter of a full bladder at two in the morning.

Despite the inconveniences, you adjust to the rigors and, if given a chance, will come to appreciate the challenges that confronting your limits will evoke.

On our third day we reached Caribou Barren, named for the long-departed woodland caribou. The sun had left, along with any sign of a trail, and light snow had begun to fall, dancing and swirling to the tune of the wind. Across the open plain the opposite border was a faint ragged line, which soon vanished entirely as a featureless curtain blended sky into land. With our hoods and scarves securely in place, we entered the enveloping storm, our compass leading the way, soon losing sight of the world in a faceless fury.

All afternoon it blew as we traversed the seemingly endless barren. There was little slide in our gait as our progress languished against the headwind. What was initially a soft powder had turned to gritty crystal, which stung exposed skin. We could barely see through our protective glasses—although there was little to see.

Eventually a scattering of trees appeared and the temperature began to rise. The snowfall tapered off and it was apparent that rain was on the way. Behind us, in the distance, stood the western fringe of the barren. We had reached the midway point of our trek and the fantasy was over. We now had to cope with the reality of setting up camp before the deluge.

But we were lucky. We spent that evening in the quasi-luxury of a tiny park shelter. It had been a task to locate it among the ragged remnants of the forest, but by the time the sky opened up, we had hauled our gear and ourselves inside. After stringing our clothes over the wood stove, we prepared a multi-course supper, and then settled down to our books and journals while sheets of water buffeted the metal roof.

By the morning of the fourth day the storm had subsided, but so had our precious powder snow. Our previously spotless terrain was now littered with debris. When we arrived at the base of White Hill we ditched our packs and took a gentle detour up the slope. A survey marker was all that differentiated the top from the surrounding terrain. But at 1,750 feet we were standing on the summit of Nova Scotia.

By late afternoon we were back into the woods and picked up the trail. However, the temperature was falling and the moist snow was quickly turning to crusty ice. Our skis lost their grip and frequent falls resulted in a broken pole and ski tip, as well as bruised egos. We were tired, wet, and moody. By the time we set up camp and crawled into our sleeping bags, the thermometer read minus twenty.

On the morning of the last day I didn't want to get up. I had slept poorly, the chill creeping into my bag throughout the night. Like a cold hand, it would jolt me awake just as I dozed off. As uncomfortable as that had been, my white breath rising to become icicles on the inner roof reminded me that it was even worse outside.

We crawled out of our shelter, clothed in bulky down jackets and booties, and fumbled through breakfast. We dallied little. It was the coldest yet and the swaying of the treetops foretold a wind chill factor that would make it much worse once we were out in the open.

Those last eight kilometres were strenuous and at times painful, especially when we broke into a clearing and a raw wind sought out every patch of exposed skin. We had to watch each other for signs of frostbite—those telltale white spots. Blowing snow crept through my scarf and clung to my beard, hanging with the frozen breath.

The trail was now almost solid ice and we plodded along toward our destination, keeping our engines fired with chocolate, granola, and juice, which had to be stored inside our jackets to keep from freezing. We stopped infrequently, since any pause allowed the cold to infiltrate our clothing. Eventually we linked up with the main park trail and dropped toward Ingonish, the coastal panorama reappearing through breaks in the hardwood cover. Familiar sounds of rural Nova Scotia returned.

At the end of our wilderness adventure we were exhausted. But Dave from Parks Canada had ferried the car around and with it some clean, dry clothes—the first in almost a week. We changed, had a hot coffee, and then it was back to Halifax and reality.

THE MAN WHO HATED WINTER
Alden Nowlan

On the days of the people who are gone, there lived a great warrior who hated winter.

During the summer, this warrior was the happiest man in his village, but when winter came he was never seen to smile. Sometimes his anger was so great that he stood at the door of his wigwam and shook his fist in the face of the north wind. Often as he walked through the village he kicked at the snow as though it were the body of a treacherous enemy.

So great, in fact, was his hatred of cold and ice and snow that some believed his spirit was possessed by those who fly through the air, or that he had made some strange pact with those who whistle in the dark. But he was terrible in battle and a mighty hunter, so men feared him and let him live.

Now, at first the god of winter was amused by the warrior's antics. Once or twice he pinched the man's nose or ears with his icy fingers to make him even more furious. "Poor little man," the god laughed, "he is like a rabbit who becomes enraged with a bear." But as time went on, the god began to lose patience.

When the god came home to his wigwam after a hard day's work of scattering snow over the world, his wife would ask him what he had done that day to chasten the mortal who defied him. And when he could not answer her, she smiled to herself—one of those mocking feminine smiles that make even the gods uneasy.

ALDEN NOWLAN

When spring came and the ice broke up in the rivers and floated down to sea, our warrior would not wait for the sun to melt the ice cakes left behind on the intervals. The people were amazed to see him attack the cakes with his war club, smash them to pieces, and hurl the pieces into the river.

One day while the warrior was destroying the ice cakes, the god of winter determined to teach the unruly mortal a lesson he would never forget. Seizing the largest ice cake he could find, the god hurled it at the mortal so he was knocked into the icy river. Then, shouting his war cry, the god leapt into the water and closed his hands around his enemy's throat.

But, unhappily for the god, it was almost spring and his strength had begun to fail him. The warrior was able to break the god's grip and swim ashore, leaving the god so exhausted that had he not succeeded in climbing on a floating ice cake he might have drowned. And to add to his discomfiture as he floated away, the warrior stood on the bank and pelted him with ice and stones.

"Be off!" cried the warrior. "Be off and never come back!" And the people of the village laughed to see their old adversary dance and tear his hair in rage as he sought to avoid the missiles hurled at him by the warrior. But the warrior did not leave off pelting the god until the little island of ice on which he stood floated around a bend in the river and disappeared from sight.

The villagers did not laugh for long, however. They knew winter would not rest until he had his revenge. That night the people sat in council and decided the warrior who had humiliated the god should be banished.

"Winter will return," the people reminded the warrior, "and when he returns he will surely kill you. If we allow you to remain among us, we and our children will also die."

So our rash warrior was sent off alone into the forest.

Summer came and it did not seem that it would ever end. While the sun smiled and the land was green, the warrior forgot his hatred of winter. Nor did he pine for his old village. He was content to wander alone through the forest and spend whole days lying in open places where the hands of the sun god caressed his body.

But when the leaves began to fall and there was need for a fire at night, he remembered the warning the villagers had given him. Yes, winter would return as he always did—and this time he would attack in the fullness of his strength; there would be no limit to his rage.

"I will sell my life dearly," vowed the warrior. And he began to arm himself for the battle that lay ahead.

First, he built a wigwam bigger than any ever before seen upon Earth. Then he cut more logs than any man had ever cut before, split the logs into firewood, and piled the firewood in his wigwam. He fashioned a mighty bow, a great stack of arrows, and a great axe with a handle of stone. He killed moose and bears and brought their skins to his wigwam.

From the day when the first snow fell, he waited for the time when winter would come to exact his revenge. So he was not surprised when the day came that the god began to beat upon the walls of his wigwam.

"What, old fool? Would you have me trounce you a second time?" sneered the warrior. He painted the sign of the sun god on his forehead, the sign of the fire god on his cheeks, and the sign of the lightning bird upon his chest—and did not forget to throw more wood on his fire.

Soon the god, using his great war axe, succeeded in cutting a hole in the wall of the warrior's wigwam. When the warrior saw the god's face peering in, he put an arrow to his bow.

"Are you fool enough to think an arrow can wound me?" laughed the god.

And his laughter was such that the wigwam shook, but the warrior was not afraid: before releasing his arrow, he set fire to it. Seeing this, the god ceased laughing and drew back. But he was not quite quick enough and the flaming arrow struck him in the shoulder.

"Now which of us is the fool?" demanded the warrior. And he smiled grimly as he heard winter rolling in the snow to heal the wound caused by the flaming arrow.

If we were to tell all that happened during the battle that followed, our tale would never end. It is said that for an entire season winter neglected the rest of the world, so intent was he on punishing the defiant warrior.

The god fought with javelins of ice and the man retaliated with burning shafts. Many times the god fought his way into the wigwam only to be driven back by the man's stone-handled axe, the blade of which he had left in the fire until it became red-hot.

Once, the god succeeded in stealing into the wigwam while the warrior slept, only to fall into a trap that sent him sprawling into the fire, which all but killed him.

The warrior did not dare to leave his wigwam for fear the god would ambush him where there was no fire. But he did not starve— for the animals, who also hated winter, came to his wigwam willingly that he might eat them and live.

As the months passed, the adversaries grew weary. Both bore innumerable wounds. But as spring approached, the god was no more certain of victory than he had been when he felt the first of the warrior's flaming arrows.

One day he came to the door of the wigwam and told the warrior he wished to speak with him.

"We have fought long enough," he said. "I come to talk of peace."

"Come in, then," answered the warrior, "but be sure you are planning no tricks, for nothing would give me greater pleasure than to pierce your heart with a flaming arrow or cut off your head with my red-hot axe blade."

Winter entered the wigwam and seated himself as far as possible from the fire.

"Of course, I could kill you in time," said the god. "But I have other matters to occupy my attention. Do you know I no longer have time to freeze more than half the rivers in the world? Because of our quarrel many parts of the forest are bare of snow. My wife scolds me. My children complain that their friends tell them I am no more than half a god. My greatest rival, the god of summer, snickers behind my back."

The warrior began to feel a little pity for his old enemy. "Your state is a sad one," he conceded.

"But what would you have me do? Surely, you can't expect me to give up my life that you may maintain your pride?"

The god sighed and tried to move still farther away from the fire.

"I ask only that you cease to make men and gods laugh at me," said he.

"And I ask only that you leave me in peace," replied the warrior.

So at last it was agreed between them.

Never again did the warrior hold winter up to ridicule and never again did winter trouble the warrior. As long as the warrior lived—and it is said that he lived to be a very old man—he was never bothered by cold, ice, or snow. It was never necessary for him to don warm robes or leggings. All year around he wore only a loincloth. And while all the rest of the world shivered in the grip of winter, the great warrior would lie on a green hillside in the bright sunlight and smell the flowers.

DREAMS THRIVE IN THE COLD
David Abbass

*D*reams thrive in the cold, on pitch-dark nights, on backyard sheets of ice lit by spotlights and kitchen windows. They move, take shape, find detail and colour, often in stripes, gain speed, breathless speed, and are launched.

First you need a few cold days, really cold days, the kind of days that made your mother, but no one else, fear for your lungs: "Pull your scarf up and remember to breathe through your nose. It's wicked cold out. Now say your morning offering and get going."

Sweet Jesus, I love you. I offer you my prayers, works, joys, and sufferings of this day. I'd offer a lot more if I could stay home.

On the trudge to school, maybe after a few drags on an imaginary cigar from a mittened hand, one might turn to the other and say: "It's probably cold enough to build a rink. For sure it is."

The pace would pick up, the trudge would quicken to a hunched trot with sliding strides across any patch of ice or hard-packed snow. We were Jean Béliveau, Frank Mahovlich, or Bobby Hull with a huge slapshot if we weren't carrying books. Gump Worsley in nets could make us late for school.

From the cheering crowds of the Forum in Montreal or Maple Leaf Gardens in Toronto, or even the Forum in Halifax where the Blackhawks and Rangers played an exhibition game that my father took me to, we'd arrive at school. Game ended.

We'd enter the holding yard and then the cheerless red brick building that was our jail for most of the sun-filled hours from

September to June, take off our coats, boots, hats, and scarves, then shuffle to our places, to our restraining devices.

The teacher talked about something, pointed to something, filled the blackboard with something.

I'd prop a pencil in my hand, hover it over a page in my scribbler, make a face as if I were thinking, cock my head slightly, and then stare out the window. The old janitor shovelling steps was fascinating, spellbinding, a parade of farting clowns compared to anything that might be said or written at the front of the class. I would study his technique, one step after another, note if he missed a spot, and whether he went back to get it. Most of all I would envy his being outside, free of the unnatural, dream-stifling heat of the classroom.

"Is it getting hot? Are you feeling too hot to think? I'll take that as a yes. Let's open a transom," our teacher might say.

Half of the transoms didn't work, but those that did were celebrated, maybe with a cheer.

"Let's settle down. You've all seen snow before."

A wisp of snow from the sill was a miraculous joy, and a reminder that it was rink weather. The teacher and whatever she was talking about didn't matter.

From my seat in the fourth row, third from the back, I would pace out our backyard, taking note of high points and low points where I'd have to pile and level snow. I'd pull the hose from the basement, give the yard a good soak, then tramp out the rink one frigid, sloshing boot-width after another, one steady, creeping row after another.

It would be great to have boards, just something to bounce pucks off and stop them from going into the snow. That would have been something to think about before the cold set in and the ground turned to granite. Back then we were too busy riding bikes, playing war, eating Halloween candy, or circling things in the Eaton's catalogue. We might pause to think of it, briefly, maybe when climbing over a pile of lumber in the garage while searching for a lost baseball, football, or baby carriage wheel if we happened to be building a buggy. The rink before was a thousand years ago and the next rink was a thousand weekends away, hardly real, more a feeling than something to plan for.

A rink without boards would have to do. I'd have it built, would have laced up my skates and shot a few pucks before the buzzer sounded and I awoke from school for the day. Freed from the classroom into the hall, we'd race without running to grab our things and make for the light, the faint glimmer that was left of it, like deep-sea divers straining for the surface. With the first few drags of fresh, cold air our blood and thoughts would flow again.

Free to run, we would, for a few clomping strides, adjust our books under our arms, catch our breath, and run some more. The snowbanks that spilled into the sidewalk, the boulder-sized chunks thrown up by plows, even the puck-sized pieces of ice—all irresistible amusements in the morning—were frustrating obstacles when we were in a hurry. Still, the twenty-five-minute walk to school could be covered in fifteen minutes on the way home, when we had a purpose.

"I'm going to build a rink!" I'd yell over my shoulder to the friends I passed and anyone I thought I knew.

Mom didn't mind that I chucked my books down just inside the kitchen door, that I kept my boots on crashing down the stairs to the basement, and that I trashed the furnace room looking for the hose and my Dad's old snow boots, the bigger the better. Feeding the hose through the dryer vent and hooking it to the washing room basin required some explanation, but not much. The outdoor tap was frozen solid.

"I'll put everything back. Everything will be fine. Don't worry," was all the reassurance my mother needed.

Building a rink is far removed from rules meant to keep homework on track, kitchen floors clean, and storm doors un-slammed. This is because parents, as much as their children, wish rinks into existence. They remove barriers, lend encouragement, and follow progress. This makes rink building more akin to mountain climbing than to play; more of an expedition with a goal and something important at stake.

Certainly it was hard, even dangerous work, alone in the frozen arctic expanse that stretched from the trees at the back of the yard to the wooden steps leading to the kitchen door, and from the fallen-down slate stone wall on one side to the bird feeder on the other.

In the beginning the spraying and stamping don't seem to lead to much—just slush and knobby foot prints. The yard looked better under a layer of snow. You might feel like quitting, like turning back. You might even be heading back to base when you feel a crunch under foot, and, with each step, the flattened translucence becomes the base of your rink now revealed.

Hope.

More flooding and tramping, and within as little as two nights you could be skating, perhaps just in one corner, or two corners connected by a smooth bit in the middle. But by this stage success is assured, as long as the weather holds.

From then on, each time you step in the house you do so as a returning hero, brave genius engineer with tales that would have captivated the builders of the pyramids, the Aztec canals, or the Colosseum in Rome.

After a few more floodings and freezings, perhaps after forming up a ridge at the edge of some low point, the rink is gleaming. It is a natural wonder in your backyard, calling out to be skated on, not in words but in a thousand urgent thoughts that come at once and blow you around like a spider in a windstorm—or a boy in boots on ice.

"Mom! I need my sweater! Where's the puck we use to keep the hall door open? Dad, are my skates sharp enough?"

Your Canadiens sweater—which was everywhere when you were looking for your bathing suit in summer—got tired of waiting. The puck has a new job somewhere, or has rolled into retirement under a bed or chest of drawers. The skates are fine. The best you could get in the kids' shoes section at Simpsons: black and brown with pale yellow laces.

The neighbourhood kids who liked to watch and sneer, and laughed when you sprayed your face unfreezing the nozzle, have managed to find *their* sweaters, skates, pucks, even a net made of two-by-fours and broken hockey sticks. If you don't hurry one of them, or his little sister, who is already lacing up, will be first on the ice.

There will be room for all, and every kid will skate and play and get a chance to push the old plow with the curled up corners, and then the broom, or else they won't be allowed back on the ice the next day. No one would risk that. I'll work the hose. I'll stay out late snaking streams through the clear, spot-lit night, deep in the corners and a little bit more over there. I'll give a final hissing mist close by my feet, then shoot one last steady blast as high as it will go and wait for it to smack the ice into perfect stillness. Then I'll climb the back steps, blow smoke rings into the steaming light, make shadows and hockey sticks dance, then leave my glorious rink in deep chill darkness for the warmth of our kitchen and the sounds of Hockey Night in Canada coming from the basement.

But now it's time to move! To strain and whirl! To smack pucks and yell! The first skate on this pristine slab goes to its builder, if he hurries.

"Do you need help with your skates?" my dad might offer as I shoulder through the back door. No time, and anyway I can tie my own skates now.

Dads like to tie skates, ask if they're tight enough, and give a few tips about deflecting pucks or getting down low in your stride, like they're passing on family secrets. We'll do that later, over and over, if it stays cold. We'll tape sticks, and he'll tell me I'll be in the NHL someday if I work hard enough.

"Skate hard, keep your head up and always keep your stick on the ice. Somebody has to play in the NHL, why not you?" he'd say up close through the rolled up band of my red, blue, and white woollen cap.

With a last pull of the laces and a flying, flourishing knot, I was two inches taller and eye-to-eye with every hockey player who ever played the game.

I'd take my stick, feel its weight, and with one explosive stride, burst through the boards to a roaring crowd in Montreal onto the blinding, snow-trimmed, silver-and-grey marvel that once was our backyard. I would skate circles, pass pucks, maybe catch Gump napping with a slapshot or send him sprawling with some spinning move. I was Jean Béliveau, Frank Mahovlich, and Bobby Hull. I was a hockey player. *La première étoile!* The first star.

There are no half-made dreams on a backyard rink. They move, take shape, find detail and colour, often in stripes, gain speed, breathless speed, and are launched, forever.

CHRISTMAS EVE CALL
Charlotte and Dan Ross

*T*his was no picture-book Christmas Eve with snow-draped pine trees and large lazy flakes drifting slowly to give a fresh covering of white to the hilly ribbon of road. It had started to snow that morning, but by mid-afternoon it had turned to a driving cold rain that left a treacherous ice coating on all it touched.

The car lay at a drunken angle—its headlights beaming skyward. His mind was numbed by the flashing action of that short second: the helpless spinning across the road's wet icy surface; the winging sensation when the wheels shot away from the gravel embankment; the jolting, sickening violence of the crash. And now—sudden quiet.

What had been a late-evening emergency call to Norton only a short time before was now a dreaded dream, and, as in a distressing dream, Dr. Paul Farrow found himself fighting through smothering clouds of fog to reality. He kept seeing the flickering flares set out at the bottom of the long hill and the big fawn truck sprawled across the road, blocking his way completely. Somehow he had to stop.

He'd fought panic and had set out to brake his car in gentle thrusts, but the moment he applied pressure to the pedal, the car had gone into a violent whirl. And now this terrifying dream again. But this time with a difference: as he looked around him, he realized his nightmare had at last come true. His immediate thought was of the emergency case waiting for him, Miller's little girl. Leaning back from the wheel he fumbled along the seat for his bag. Then he stared blankly out the car window.

The car, he sensed, was wedged in a ditch, well below the level of the icy road. Great beads of perspiration broke out all over him, and he felt nauseated and weak. He knew he was not hurt except perhaps for a few bruises. He hated to think of it, but the only thing that held him there helpless was his own cowardice. He knew he would never find the courage to drive on to Norton over that treacherous glaze. Not even if it meant giving his friend's child a chance to live.

He had always dreaded driving on wet ice, ever since that winter night when he had helped lift his father's broken body from the car.

Three weeks ago he had found an excuse to avoid going to old Mrs. Williams when she had taken one of her heart spells during a nighttime sleet storm. He remembered the expression on his wife's face the night he had hesitated in going out to the Hennessey boy, suddenly stricken with appendicitis. Only that look of Ethel's had made him venture on that dangerous back road.

He was thankful that tonight Ethel and their four-year-old Marie were safe in the city visiting Ethel's parents. The storm had made the roads a deadly trap and she'd phoned earlier to say she'd not drive home until the morning, even though Marie's Christmas tree was lighted and waiting in a corner of the living room.

Later, as he'd sat in the warm glow of the tree's lights, the phone again broke the room's quiet. He had waited for a moment, considering whether he should answer it. Then, ashamed at his hesitation, he picked up the receiver.

The line had been noisy, and Farrow had just been able to make out: "Playing with matches...little girl...burned badly!" in Miller's familiar voice, strained with tension. Then they had been completely cut off.

Desperately seeking courage, he had stood there for a few minutes. Strange that it should be Miller's child. The Millers were close friends. His own Marie often played with the freckle-faced youngster who had been burned. He had reluctantly put on his coat and prepared his bag for the dreaded drive.

There was still another reason why he must not fail in his duty tonight. Miller knew about Farrow's personal agony. They had discussed it one evening.

"Believe me, Paul," Miller had said solemnly, "all of us have some special phobia or weakness. Each man has to face up to his own and conquer it. If you don't lick it, it will eventually lick you. Stop running away from your fear, and one day you'll smile at the memory of it."

"Thanks—for no help at all," Farrow answered bitterly.

"Your help lies within you," Miller had ended.

So now he was faced with it: the nightmare, the dream that had haunted him. His lips moved in silent prayer, not for himself but for the Miller child out there waiting for his aid, the aid he was not man enough to give. He wondered if there was anyone down ahead with the truck. Had they noticed him when he went off the road?

He stood outside the car in the beating rain. Then he slowly stumbled up the embankment to the roadway. He hesitated there in the downpour and peered ahead at the flickering red flares still outlining the truck in an eerie glow. Help would have to come quickly to Miller's child if it was to do any good.

Perhaps the line to Belleisle Creek was still in order. He might get a call through to old Dr. Halliday. It was possible he could drive to Norton from the other direction and treat the little girl in time. Yes, he'd locate a phone and explain the situation to Halliday. Carefully picking his steps along the slush-covered shoulder, he started down in the direction of the transport. He felt better now that he had a plan.

Finally coming to the truck, he charted a path across the treacherous road surface, now rose-coloured, reflecting the danger flares. As he reached the cab, the door swung open, and a familiar figure jumped down. It was Len Underhill, who owned a nearby farm and was a patient of his.

"Doc Farrow!" There was surprise and concern in Len's tone.

"This is a bad way for you to spend Christmas Eve! No kind of a night to be on the road!"

He nodded in grim agreement. "I know. On my way to Norton—emergency call—ditched my car on the top of the hill." He tried to sound brusque and casual.

"That's bad!" Rivulets of rain dripped from Len's cap down over his forehead and cheeks. "I saw the lights come up over the hill and then shoot away. I thought somebody was off the road but I'm not able to leave this thing until the driver gets back. He's at my place now callin' a tow truck."

"Then the line to Belleisle Creek is working!" Farrow said eagerly. Then checking himself, he went on in careful explanation: "The little Miller girl has been badly burned, she needs attention. I'll never get there now, but I thought Dr. Halliday might be able to drive down."

Len shook his head doubtfully. "Not likely tonight, Doc. He hasn't been makin' night calls since he was sick last summer. And with the roads as they are now, I don't think he'd ever get there."

Len glanced down and scuffed the softening ice with a heavy boot. "Road will be clear in a couple of hours, but that would be too late."

Then he glanced up at Farrow and his face brightened. "I tell you what, Doc. You take my car. She's over there in the driveway and full of gas."

He stood trapped and helpless inside his own terrified flesh. He struggled to keep back the panic rising in him, as he faltered with: "No! No! I couldn't do that! I've wrecked one car tonight—I—"

He turned away.

"That's okay, Doc," Len smiled reassuringly. "Couldn't hurt that old heap of mine. Anyhow, there's only a couple more real bad spots between here and Norton." Then he became solemn. "Besides, I know what it means to be waiting for the doctor. And I can guess how you feel when folks are alone out there depending on you."

Folks alone out there depending on you!

Len's words echoed through Farrow's fear. And they did something to him—strangely, he felt a new sensation of calm. He saw his plight in its true perspective. He had the choice of two roads: one led to Norton and Miller's injured child, the other to defeat and the shameful suicide of his decency. There was no reason to hesitate any longer; he had made his decision.

His jaw set, he held out his hand. "Give me the keys," he said quietly.

Many times during the next half-hour Farrow's newfound resolution almost deserted him but he kept on driving, slowly, painfully. He fixed his eyes on the road ahead, not daring to look at the embankments. One numbing moment on Full Mile Hill the car swerved wildly, but he fought back, forcing himself to hold on to the wheel and guide the vehicle through the danger. Now he slowly headed the car into the Miller's rutted driveway. He had made the drive only because he had willed it.

When Miller opened the front door and saw him, his tired face flooded with relief.

"You made it!" he said with meaning.

Farrow nodded. "How is she?"

Miller took his dripping hat and coat. "Resting more easily, Paul," he said. "Bad enough but she'll be all right now that you're here. She's in there with her mother." He pointed to the closed door at the end of the hall.

Farrow started toward it, but as he passed the open archway to the living room he stopped. He stared at Mrs. Miller, sitting on the davenport, her arm around her little girl, who was huddled sleepily against her.

He turned to Miller. "I don't understand."

Miller showed surprise and stammered, "But—I—told you."

"The line was noisy—we were cut off," Farrow told him tautly.

"But you understood about the matches—the accident?" He paused. "You see Ethel stopped here on her way home. She was trying to make it because of Christmas Eve but the storm...you surely knew it was your Marie who...."

Farrow saw the bedroom door open and Ethel came out. She ran to his arms with a sob of relief. He held her close for a brief second of tenderness.

"It will be all right," he whispered.

Then, without fear, he went through the doorway to the bedside of his child.

ICE MAGIC

Gary Saunders

*T*he Inuit, we are told, have more than thirty names for what to us is ordinary snow. Linguists and anthropologists make much of this fact. But I am sure that Down East motorists have just as many names for ice, only most of them are unprintable here. And little wonder. After enduring five or six months a year of what newscasters blithely call "occasional icy patches" or "intermittent freezing rain" or the like; after fishtailing and skidding about the highways times without number, narrowly missing this object or that precipice (and sometimes not), what could one expect?

The other morning while scraping knobby ice from my car windows for the tenth time this month, I was moved to reflect on how the quality of ice has sunk since I was a youngster. I couldn't help but note that the hard material I was endeavoring to dislodge bore hardly any resemblance to the substance I remembered from childhood. The stuff under my scraper seemed to be of some common grade, rough and unfriendly; not at all like the magical and somehow amiable ice I recalled. While this kind mocked my efforts and spoiled my morning, the other kind would put a catch in my breath as I scrambled into my windbreaker on a bright Saturday at sun-up....

Perhaps being wealthy helped—wealthy in ice. I mean, most years we had a whole Newfoundland bay of it. This must have given our parents nightmares but to us it was sheer pleasure. The two best seasons were when the ice was either making or breaking. And of the two, the making season held more magic.

Normally the ice started to make around December. We knew it was near when we woke and saw frost ferns on our bedroom windows. As soon as I was let out I would head for the nearest ditch or puddle. If it looked strong enough I would jump up and down on it; otherwise a rock would tell me how thick it was without the risk of wet feet.

One thing that always puzzled me was how the ice formed in the first place. Often at dusk after a thaw I would squat and try to see it actually *happening*. First there was just the dark water shivering a little, and then, out of nowhere, came these little tapered transparent points, straight on one side and feathered on the other, reaching out over the quivery surface from all sides. But they never did anything while I watched. They were either there or not there. Yet come back the next morning and the process was complete, the crystal matrix all interlocked and patiently cross-braced with triangular struts like a geodesic dome. Very mysterious.

Just as mysteriously, after a few false starts, the whole bay would catch over from shore to shore, freezing first in the coves and between islands, and finally down the centre where the river current ran. By January or February the ice could bear a team of horses with a load of logs. Then we didn't need permission any more.

Skates were scarce in Newfoundland around 1945. We didn't seem to miss them much. One of our favourite games was a kind of ice boating. You simply took your sled to a lee shore on a windy day, stuck a nice bushy fir or spruce as big as you could handle between your knees, and shoved off. Man, could that sled go! Skimming across the glare ice as free as gulls, slicing through scattered snowdrifts in puffs of white like summer clouds, careening onto one runner as we tried to steer clear of a frozen knob of horse manure, or each other.

The only trouble was getting back. The ideal conditions for this sport came when a frontal system dumped enough rain to coat the bay with new ice, and left a bitter westerly gale in its wake. However, east for us was away from home, which meant a long walk back against a stiff wind. For better footing, some of us fashioned "creepers" of nails in blocks of wood, modelled after the metal ones the old ladies wore when they ventured out to Divine Service in the winter.

One Sunday morning, in an ecstasy of speed like Johnathan L. Seagull's, I ended up several miles out the bay, alone. It seemed a long, lonely trek back. Hearing the accusing chimes of morning service pealing across the ice did not help.

More mundane but just as delightful was smelting. We thought we invented it. Certainly our equipment was primitive: a piece of kindling at one end with enough shop twine to reach bottom, a couple of small trout hooks, and a piece of salt beef or pork for bait. Plus the coaster, a box to put the fish in, an axe, and a lunch. On reaching the right place we went ashore and cut boughs to kneel on and enough small trees to stop the wind and make it dark enough to see the smelts through the ice.

When all was complete there was this very cozy feeling; no wind, a nice shelter, and down there, maybe, those lithe, silvery little fishes. Half the fun was in peering down into their dim world where olive-green eel grass undulated in the tide like timothy in a summer breeze, and where every pebble and blue mussel shell was clearly visible. If all went well we would have smelts for supper.

There were some hazards. Ballicators were one. Ballicators could swallow a good-sized child or even a man if one accidentally stepped in them. Ballicators (my spelling may be incorrect; it isn't in the dictionary) appeared where the ice had pyramided over a rock at low tide and frozen in the form of a volcano. They rose and fell with the tides, and some of them had open tops. Sometimes we slid down their steep sides.

Another hazard was rents. Rents were fissures caused by expansion. The ones along the shore were the worst, because they often let in water on a rising tide, blocking our way to shore. The offshore ones usually stayed frozen and were said to be safe. But we never really trusted them, because now and then they would boom like a cannon under our feet and scare us silly.

It was years before I connected our seemingly peculiar use of the word "rent" with the word used in the King James Bible to express extreme remorse: "he rent his garments." The bay was simply rending its too-tight garment of ice.

If the coming of the ice was the more magical event, its leave-taking was the more thrilling. This was due to "Copying Pans," a game that entailed trotting across a stretch of water (preferably deep and wide) on an assemblage of flatting ice pans (preferably small). The first to get wet was out; the last to finish dry-shod was winner.

During the spring breakup we copied pans before and after school and during recess. One day I decided to take the next logical step and use a pan for travelling to and from school—a quarter-mile walk. I reckoned the distance was shorter by sea. After lunch, I selected a pole—a nice piece of edging from the slab pile near my uncle's sawmill—and went down to the shore to pick the most boat-like pan I could find. Then I set out across the broad cove.

From the start the pan was surprisingly hard to push. It was also hard to keep on a straight course. When I ran to one end to turn it, that end would start to dive like a submarine. My deck was soon awash and slippery. Worse, in my efforts to navigate I lost bottom and began to drift.

Now I had a moment of panic: if a wind came up I might be blown offshore and be carried out of the bay by the steady current. Then I remembered that a pole could be used as a makeshift paddle. By sculling and threshing about, I finally managed to regain the shallow water and beach my crazy craft. The scare kept me on dry land for a whole week.

Copying Pans marked the end of the major ice events in our year. The next thing we knew, there were only a few pans left, stranded along the shore like beached whales and dripping in the suddenly warm sun. Even the remnants of snowbanks were too sugary for a decent snowball. This might have troubled us, except that already the almost-forgotten smell of wet mud was steaming out from under the shrinking drifts. Already the small brooks in the woods sang of trouting and swimming, and the barn-soiled sheep, heavy with lamb, were out searching for the first blades of green. It was spring.

Spring took our minds off the ice.

Although the quality of ice has declined a great deal since I was a youngster, this at least has not changed: spring still takes my mind off it.

Hurry up, spring.

NO GIRLS ALLOWED
Monica Graham

*N*o Girls Allowed. The caretakers wasted no paint emblazoning the words all over my town's hockey rink, because everyone already knew the rule.

The exception, of course, was Friday nights, when a record player belted scratchy waltzes into the crisp air. The prettier girls got invited by brave and agile boys to dance around the ice, while the adventurous ones played crack the whip, a game in which speed overtook ability and allowed participants to crash satisfactorily into the waltzing couples.

Girls could also skate for two hours on Saturday afternoons, when small screeching children spent most of their time sliding across the ice on the reinforced knees of their snow pants. Racing, waltzing, and games of crack the whip were forbidden. Round and round in boring circles, first one way, and then another. The experience cost a whole quarter, and it was enough to make any sensibly adventurous girl want to go home to knit.

Not only were girls restricted to five hours of skating a week, we also had to wear white figure skates. It didn't matter that not a single one of us had ever attempted a figure eight or a pirouette. Girls had to wear white figure skates—albeit with the picks filed off the toes— and that was that. Later, an Eaton's catalogue showcased baby-blue figure skates. A couple of trendsetters persuaded their parents they couldn't live without them, but it didn't take long for the blue to get covered with white shoe polish. We had never heard of long-bladed racing skates but if we had, we wouldn't have worn them. They looked too much like hockey skates, and girls just were not allowed.

The ice belonged to the boys. On calm, cold days I could hear them from my backyard, three blocks away. I could hear their hoarse yells, the smack of sticks on pucks, the *sksshh sksshh* of their skates, and the scraping sound as the black rubber slid towards goal. I knew the *clack-clack-clack* of their sticks on the ice was a signal: "Pass me the puck! Look, I'm open! Pass it to me!" I could hear their anger when someone broke the rules they had created: no lifting the puck, no picking on the little guys, no fighting. I could hear their cheers when someone scored.

Dad spent many a Saturday morning spraying water in our backyard so we could have our own rink. But gently lobbing pucks at my little brother crouched between the two blocks of firewood that stood for goal posts was not the same as the rough-and-tumble game down the street.

I wanted to play hockey so badly it hurt.

I got my wish when my grade four teacher moved Kenny into the seat in front of me. Shorter and more cheerful than me and covered in freckles, he spent most of his time turned around earnestly discussing hockey with me. There were just six teams in the NHL then, and he knew the stats of every single player. Our chats were likely not the outcome the teacher envisioned when she moved Kenny from the rowdy back row, but they gave me the chance to play hockey.

I confided my dream to Kenny, and we cooked up a plan.

Most of the other boys in his neighbourhood attended a different school, so he figured they wouldn't know me if I suddenly arrived to play hockey with them on Saturday morning. No one would ask questions about his new friend from school.

My younger brother had a pair of used hockey skates handed down from an older cousin, but they were too big for him. I decided I would wear them, along with my brother's jacket, stocking cap, and mitts. No one would know I was a girl.

That Saturday dawned bright and bitterly cold. I told my parents I'd been invited to play hockey, a statement they accepted with ease, even eagerness. Possibly they recognized my yearning to play. I didn't tell them I would have to pretend to be a boy.

Mom never questioned when I raided my little brother's gear, and borrowed his new Boy Scout quilted jacket, purchased two sizes too big for him so he would grow into it. But she laid down the law when I started out of the house with no long johns, having discovered my brother's were too short.

It was close to minus twenty on the Fahrenheit scale, so she ordered me to put on my tan cable-knit tights under my snow pants. She didn't know those tights would have to be hidden when I changed from my boots, which, thankfully, were buckle-up galoshes worn by boys and girls alike.

Skates slung over my brother's hockey stick, stick slung over my shoulder, I almost danced to the rink.

Unlike Friday nights and Saturday afternoons, there was no glowing fire in the rink shack's potbellied stove, no music, no canteen, and the building itself was as cold as a grave. Kenny said a casual hello, and indicated that I should perch on the icy bench next to him to change into my stiff, frozen skates. Careful not to expose my dainty cable-knit legs, I hauled on my brother's hand-me-down skates and tightened the laces.

The players ran the gamut from tiny ferocious six-year-olds to lanky teens with the beginnings of beards. Soon we drew up two fairly evenly matched teams with far too many players per side, but who cared? We all had ice time.

Unfortunately (from my point of view), I ended up on the team opposite Kenny's. At least I wasn't the last one picked.

My captain was a tall blond boy with acne and a love of checking his opponents—even his own teammates. He was allowed to do that. We had no referee. If any blue or red lines were ever painted on the ice, they had long been obscured by weeks of skate scars and flooding with a fire hose. The teams verbally settled their differences over offsides and icings, and not a single penalty was called.

My memory of the actual play is limited. I remember my feet were very cold at first, but after a few minutes they stopped bothering me. I remember tearing up and down the ice, sucking the frozen air into my lungs and letting it sting my cheeks and forehead. I remember that almost no one passed me the puck, but the one time my blade did touch it I fired it at the net. It glanced off the goalie's skate, hit the inside of the goal post, and bounced out of the crease.

Pretty close for a beginner. It sparked a heated argument between the two captains, and I stood back to let them yell at each other. Whether they decided I had scored or not, my happiness was complete. I had taken a shot. When the captains finally realized I didn't care, play resumed.

But my hockey career ended about ten minutes later.

My own captain checked me as we both chased the puck, and I fell and slid across the ice and into the net. The impact hiked the leg of my snow pants up past my knee. The players nearest skidded to a stop, showering me with shredded ice. I looked up at several pairs of eyes glaring down at me. And my tan cable-knit tights.

They turned away, and started whispering among themselves as I scrambled upright. Kenny soon emerged from the huddle, his freckles merged in rosy embarrassment.

"You have to go now," he muttered. He half-turned to indicate his friends. "They don't want to play with a girl."

If then was now, I would argue. Now, I would fight for my right to play hockey. But back then, I was cold, it was lunchtime, and I'd already gotten away with three hours of illicit Saturday fun.

"It's okay," I replied. "I gotta go home anyhow."

I changed back into my frigid boots, wincing as frostbite ebbed and stabbed my feet. Trying not to visibly hobble, I gathered my brother's gear.

"G'bye!" I called to my erstwhile teammates. "Thanks! I had a real good time."

The captain skated over to the boards.

"You play pretty good...for a girl," he said.

A few days later a sudden thaw destroyed the ice surface and relieved Kenny of the discomfort of telling me for a second time that no girls were allowed. By the time the caretakers rebuilt the ice, my Saturdays were taken up with other things.

We moved to another town, one with no rink, and it was ten years before I played hockey again—this time on a university women's intramural team.

But the first time was still the best time.

THE PHANTOM DOG TEAM
Harry Paddon

*A*ll sparsely populated backcountry areas have their ghosts and Labrador, like the rest, has its fair share. The nice thing about the ghosts of Labrador is that they have kept the qualities of the old-timers of the era in which they entered the spirit world. They are a friendly, helpful group of spirits with more constructive things to do than merely to haunt the living as their more highly civilized counterparts seem to do. Instead they appear to have a protective attitude towards their still-living neighbours and descendants.

Such a one is "the Smoker" who, many times, has stuck his ethereal nose into the battering blasts of a Labrador blizzard to rescue a careless or unlucky traveller who should have known better. How the Smoker got his name I couldn't say…unless it derives from his ability to appear and vanish like a puff of smoke. Or possibly it came from the fact that his appearance always occurred on a night of smoking thick drift on the barren lands he ranged. There is no question that the many to whom he appeared—including a newly arrived and hard-boiled Hudson's Bay man who had never heard of him—firmly believe that he did indeed come to their aid, and without his help they would have surely perished.

The particular incident I wish to relate occurred some fifty years ago and, since the people involved were friends of my family, I shall take a few liberties with their names. The story shall remain theirs as they told it.

Bill and Jane Gordon's winter home lay several miles inland from their summer fishing place at Bluff Head. Chosen for the generous area of woods that had furnished logs for the comfortable house and now sheltered it from the savage winds off the rocky barrens, the winter place was an isolated spot. The nearest neighbours were two families at Rocky Cove—fifteen miles across the barren, rocky neck— and it was nearly forty miles to the trading post at Rigolet. The Neck was something to be treated with respect by winter travellers, for the way across the bare, windswept ridges was unmarked. To go astray in one of the frequent winter gales was to risk death by freezing on its pitiless miles of shelterless rocks and ice, or by plunging storm-blinded from one of its many cliffs.

A few days before Christmas, Bill and Jane left home to go to Rigolet to trade their furs and bring home a few extras from the store. Their two children, twelve-year-old Joe and little Janet, ten, were quite undismayed at the prospect of being left to fend for themselves for a night or two. Joe had considered himself a man quite some time now, for he could do a man's work in the woods or the fish stage, and he had been hunting and trapping alone for a couple of winters. Janet reckoned she could look after the house as well as any woman, and Joe, who had helped his father harness the dogs that morning, was rather looking forward to being the boss for a while. So it was with quite a holiday feeling that the youngsters watched the team fade into the distance as they speculated on what wonders its load might contain when it again came over the hill in two or three days.

A couple of hours on the easy going of the firm, wind-packed snow of the ridges brought Bill and Jane to Rocky Cove where they stopped briefly for a cup of tea and a yarn with the first of their neighbours they had not seen in two months. From Rocky Cove the way lay mostly on the ice to Rigolet and their arrival there was before sundown. Putting up at the Hudson's Bay Company's kitchen, where open house was kept for travellers, they spent the evening in visiting the few households of the tiny village and the next day settled to their trading. By the time this was finished it was too late to leave Rigolet and a second night was spent in the cheery company of friends who had not been seen for months and might not again be seen for many more. It was in the graying dawn of their third day from home that Bill lashed up his load and harnessed his team for the return trip.

When the red rim of the sun turned the sea ice to a crimson plain at the purple-shadowed feet of the hills, they were five or six miles on their way. The day promised to be fair as the frosty vapor from the panting breaths of the dogs hung in the still air. They stopped again for a brief warm-up and a snack at Rocky Cove before starting the last fifteen miles across the neck toward home. It was with a slight feeling of unease that Bill noticed the beginning of a wispy cloud formation to the east as they pulled away from Rocky Cove and began their ascent to the ridges. The evening was calm and fine, however, and he reckoned that the two-hour run to home would be safely done long before any bad weather moved in.

The only worrisome thing was that his was a young team and the year-old pup he was training to be a leader seemed to have little sense. The old leader had died last fall and could have been trusted to take them home—no matter how thick the weather—without deviating a whisker's length from the trail. Bill didn't quite know if he could trust the pup who always seemed to want to be told where to go.

It was clouding in rapidly now and though still calm, the very stillness held the menace of something waiting to pounce.

Halfway across the neck the first few snowflakes began to fall. Darkness curtained the rocky slopes as the first searching fingers of icy wind stirred the gathering powder into feathery swirls and dragged them, rustling, across the tops of the drifts. In the space of a quarter of an hour it was blowing a gale and in the black of the night, the thickening snow blotted everything from sight in a weaving wall of sound and pelting icy particles.

The dog team faltered, slowed, and stopped. The young leader had no confidence in his ability to stay on the trail, and his mates shared his uncertainty. Unable to see more than a few yards, Bill began to consider the advisability of finding a hollow sheltered enough to burrow into the snow for the night. Though this would mean a risk of freezing, it might present a better chance of survival than would be offered by blundering blindly on with a very good chance of plunging over a cliff. Already the biting wind was beginning to leave little spots of frostbite on any exposed skin; it wouldn't be long before Bill and Jane began to freeze quite badly.

Bill knew they were still on the trail, for just there, by his leader, a pyramid-shaped cairn of rocks marked where the Big Brook trail came in from the north to join their own. He walked out through the team and stood by the cairn, recalling the various folds in the nearby land that might offer shelter enough to permit them to get through this night.

As he stood, the voice of another driver reached his ears—the voice of a man urging his team onward, and, as he looked, a team surged out of the swirling darkness. Nine black and white dogs trotted by, almost near enough to touch. On the komatik behind them knelt a lone man who gestured urgently at Bill to follow before he turned again to face his team. Bill's own dogs, crazy with excitement, were already lunging into their traces. As the komatik slid by, he dropped to his seat on the load. Though the other team was a strange one, the driver seemed to know where he was going, for he drove with the assurance of a man whose leader had been over the road before.

For an hour the two teams trotted steadily through the swirling blackness, Bill's young team straining against their heavy load to let the young leader keep his nose almost touching the stern of the leading komatik. On some of the steeper grades where the weight of their load threatened to cause them to fall behind, the black team slowed a little to let them keep up. Bill marvelled at the control the stranger had over his team, for he was travelling light and could easily run them out of sight in no time. It wasn't until a faint spark of light through the storm showed where the house lay ahead that the strange team drew ahead in a burst of speed.

Back at the house Bill and Jane's youngsters had been having a grand time. Joe had had one day hunting ptarmigan on the ridges above the house. The second day he had harnessed up his own team of pups and gone out to the summer place, where a day on the ice foot by the open sea had yielded some of the big eider ducks that would make a fine Christmas dinner. Both days, with her housework done, Janet had spent some hours fishing through the ice at the mouth of the brook, and several dozen trout and a few hundred smelt had been added to the stock of frozen fish in the bins of the storehouse. The third day they both stayed close to home. From noon on many were the glances they took at the trail from the hills where their parents' team should appear any time now. The first twinges of anxiety began as the weather worsened at dusk. The coming of full darkness brought with it a wind that roared off the hills and drove icy scuds of drift rattling across the window panes. The youngsters were silently thoughtful as they sat down to supper. Both hoped the storm had struck on the other side of the neck early enough to cause their parents to stay the night at Rocky Cove.

Supper was barely over when a chorus of welcoming yelps and howls from Joe's pups brought them to their feet to stare through the windows. A team—not their father's, but a team of nine big black and white dogs—drew up to the door and stopped at a low-voiced command from the driver. Joe hastily pulled on his jacket and cap to go out and welcome the stranger. Janet watched as the dogs, in the usual fashion of a team glad to have reached the end of a hard day, rolled and rubbed their faces in the snow to rid their eyes of the accumulation of frost from their breaths. The driver stood for a moment by his komatik and coiled up his long whip as he waited for some sign from within.

As Janet watched, Joe appeared from the lean-to porch and walked into the square of lamplight from the window. The leader, a huge, powerful-looking beast, gambolled playfully toward him and Joe stooped to pull its harness off.

As he reached for the leader Joe stopped and gazed unbelieving at his hands, for there was nothing between them. There on the windswept deck he was alone, more alone than he had ever been in his life—the nine big dogs with their driver and the big tripping komatik had *vanished*.

Joe turned and started back to the door, worried by what little Janet, watching from the window, might be making of this. As he reached for the latchstring, an uproar of welcome again broke from his team of pups tethered by the edge of the woods. This time, as he turned to face whatever might be coming, it was his father's familiar team that trotted jauntily onto the lamp-lit deck.

The dogs crowded around Joe, rubbing their bodies against his legs, each frantic to draw his attention and be the next unharnessed. It wasn't until Joe had sorted out and coiled up the mass of sealskin traces that he approached the komatik to help his father unlash and carry in the load.

As he straightened from his bent position to coil the long lash-line Bill asked, "What became of the team that came in ahead of us?"

Joe hoisted a heavy sack to his shoulder and turned toward the house. "There was no team," he answered quietly.

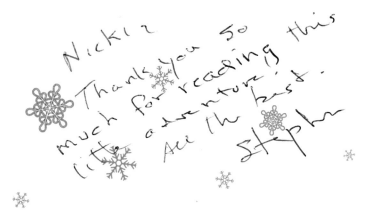

Nickie ~
Thank you so
much for reading this
little adventure!
All the best.
Stephen

ESCAPE FROM REFUGEE COVE
Steve Abbass

"Should I bring this?" I yelled, pulling a large flashlight out of the van.

"No. It's just a day hike!"

I put the light back in the van and stumbled after the others as they strode into the Chignecto wilderness.

That brief exchange now ran on a continuous loop in my brain as we felt our way through the dense coastal forest in near-total darkness. I say "the coast" but it had been some hours since we last looked down on the Bay of Fundy. And it was turning very cold. And swirls of snow had begun to sting our eyes.

"The Chignecto Wilderness Trail: even in the best conditions the going is tough. Steep climbs rewarded by treacherous descents and even more punishing ascents to forested plateaus overlooking the spectacular Bay of Fundy six hundred feet below." It was right there in the brochure.

What was I thinking? I'm not an outdoorsy kind of guy. I like sidewalks and coffee shops. I get lost walking through the Public Gardens in downtown Halifax. Why, at the tender age of forty-eight, had I decided to cut my teeth on one of the most challenging hikes Nova Scotia has to offer?

"Stick with me, pal! You have more summers behind you than ahead of you!"

The answer, of course, was my buddy Joel.

"But it's mid-December," I protested.

"Trust me, pal."

Never trust anyone who says "trust me."

Unlike myself, Joel was an avid and expert outdoorsman. He could not conceive of anyone choosing to sit behind a desk or in a café when they could be risking life and limb shooting down rapids in a canoe, scaling a cliff, or getting lost in the woods.

"Everyone will be there," he insisted.

He was also a born organizer. For years he had planned and promoted countless wilderness adventures to the delight of a small group of fellow fanatics who were ready to follow him into the abyss at a moment's notice.

Up until then, I had had the good sense not to get drawn into their madness. But Joel's haranguing finally wore me down, so I threw caution and common sense to the wind and headed out on my very first Joel Feinstein Adventure. On the menu: a demanding day hike from Red Rocks to Refuge Cove, and back along the rocky shores of the Bay of Fundy.

"Highest tides in the world, pal!"

"Should I pack a life jacket?" I asked, only half joking. Apparently the North Atlantic funnels into a space much too small for it so the water has only one place to go: up. Forty feet up.

"Got it covered, pal," assured Joel. He would check the tides in the *Halifax Daily Journal*.

I don't know why Joel was so determined that I join this group of otherwise-experienced hikers. I suppose he thought I needed to get out more. What I really needed was a cigarette to go with the Bic lighter that was now providing our only illumination as we searched high and low for a small red trail marker.

"Do you think we're lost?" Claire Turnbull asked as she shuffled beside me. Claire was an athletic blond in her mid-thirties—a serious runner out for a little cross-training.

"Nah, I'm sure we're still in Nova Scotia," I answered. I get saucy when I'm cold and tired.

She shot me an icy stare...as if it wasn't cold enough already.

"How's it looking?" I shouted through the wind to a figure barely visible up ahead.

"It's all good! Follow me!" Dave shouted back reassuringly.

Dave "Hawkeye" Tobin was now in the lead. He'd been a track star in an earlier life, and now coached football at a local university.

"Not much further now!"

A true leader of men, he had encouraged us on with a positive energy that bordered on the pathological.

"We're getting there!"

"Keep up the good work."

"You're doing great!"

"Don't fall."

As inspiring as this seemed at first, now having trudged some three hours along an increasingly hostile and unfamiliar trail, it was wearing a bit thin.

"Do you think we're lost?" Claire asked again, feeling the cold now.

"Either that or seriously misplaced." I was on a roll now.

Her silence spoke volumes.

"Aye. We gotta bushwack, laddie!" barked Sandy MacPhail as he squeezed past us to confront Joel who, to my great surprise, was still languishing at the rear.

"Do ye hear me, laddie?" He implored, stubbornly clinging to his thick Scottish brogue despite having lived in "New Scotland" for the past thirty years.

Sandy was a serious trekker. A bit too serious. He had recently summited Mount Kilimanjaro in Tanzania and now seemed to hold any lesser hike in utter contempt. I couldn't help thinking it'd be hard to get lost on Kilimanjaro—you're either going up or you're going down—but what do I know?

"We gotta bushwhack!" he persisted.

Joel shot him a glare and continued to languish.

I kept waiting for Joel to snap out of it and revert back to character. Where was the bullshit? Where was the bluster? More importantly: where were we?

And what about Joel's buddy Sid? The aging golden boy. The intrepid thrill-seeker. Had his luck finally run out? Was he desperately clinging to the Cape Chignecto cliffs? Had he been swallowed by the tide? A sense of dread had dogged every footstep as we followed this cursed path inland and lost sight of the Bay of Fundy. And what were those lights we had seen on the water? Were rescue vessels flooding the cliffs with light in search of our missing companion?

A lifetime ago we were all relaxing together on the rocks of Refugee Cove, eating our lunch and admiring the glorious vista. Having descended six hundred feet into this small-pebbled valley, we sat dwarfed by soaring cliffs and looked out on a majestic and benign Bay of Fundy only a few hundred yards away. Our gruelling three-and-a-half-hour hike had been richly rewarded.

Even in mid-December, the noonday sun flooded the protected valley, baking the rocks and creating a microclimate warm enough that Joel and his friend Sid had peeled off their shirts to bask in its unseasonable glow. Though tired and sore from the morning's hike, a feeling of intense relaxation and contentment came over me. Joel was right. This was heaven.

"Stick with me, pal."

The mood was ebullient. Even Sandy MacPhail was smiling and engaging in friendly banter.

"Awk, ye call this a hike do ye, laddie? Now Kilimanjaro, there's a hike," he teased as he tucked into his haggis sandwich.

Okay, he may not have actually said "awk" or "laddie"…and it was a ham sandwich.

It was then Sid's turn to hold court. A seasoned and flamboyant raconteur, he regaled us with tales of adventure and acts of daring-do: the time he lived in a grass hut in New Guinea, or alpine skied across the Cape Breton highlands. I found it amazing that he could draw a narrative spanning New Guinea to Cape Breton Island. But again: what do I know?

Claire wandered down the beach and started climbing the surrounding rock. Apparently the morning's exertions had not been challenging enough for her. Dave and the others, unable to resist the challenge, followed closely after her, each clambering up the rock face and drinking in the seascape from their elevated perches. Even I found an imposing rock to call my own. We were kids again.

Then, all too soon, Joel broke our reverie with an abrupt "Let's go or we'll miss the tide!"

We gathered up our day packs and prepared for the journey home along the shoreline of the Bay of Fundy. Sid caught me as I took a last look around at the unearthly beauty that surrounded us.

"Many a novice hiker has had to be rescued from these cliffs," said Sid with a mischievous twinkle in his eye.

I nodded gravely in agreement before realizing he was pulling my leg.

Gales of laughter erupted as everyone enjoyed my momentary embarrassment. A good-natured joke at the rookie's expense. Oh well. I joined in their hearty laughter and it was no longer about me. It was about life, the adventure, the air, the wind—it was about everything. I had the sense of being admitted to an exclusive club.

And then we were off. A few hours winding along the Fundy shore and we would be back in the van and headed for home. This was good. More than good—it was a true outdoor adventure! Lots of stories to impress my new fiancée. "Not such a city boy now, am I?"

The hike back along the shore was proving more difficult than I had anticipated. The footing was treacherous and uneven and I struggled to keep up. I lost sight of the others as they disappeared beyond a massive pillar of rock protruding from the cliff face. Water was lapping against the behemoth when I reached it. I clambered over only to be welcomed by another long stretch of misery, totally soaking my new hikers in the process.

I was falling farther and farther behind and my feet were wet. Why were my feet wet? Were my feet supposed to be wet? After a moment's panic, I summoned up every ounce of my long-dormant survival instinct and raced ahead.

As I approached the group, they were stopped in front of another outcropping and in the middle of a heated discussion. I was stumbling toward them, out of breath but proud of my superhuman effort, when they suddenly broke huddle and began walking toward me.

"Turn around, we're headed back." A dejected-looking Joel said, brushing past me.

"Headed back where?"

"To Refugee Cove, laddie," answered Sandy nearly bowling me over as he hurried by. This time I'm almost sure he said "laddie."

"We're taking the trail back," Dave explained, breaking into a jog.

Apparently while I was struggling to catch up, a committee had been struck that determined the tide had actually been coming in as we were basking on the rocks, not receding as we had thought. Claire had cast the deciding vote, refusing to take any chance of being trapped against the cliffs. That settled the matter as it's a well-established rule that a hiking party should never separate. We would all head back along the beach to Refugee Cove, climb back into the woods, and retrace our steps home. All except "Devil may care" Sid, who, rebellious to the end, was determined to race the tide back along the shore to Red Rocks.

"Time and tide wait for no man!" He yelled theatrically, as he vaulted over the rock face and disappeared from view.

I felt it odd that other established rules, including always bring a flashlight and compass, had already been ignored but this rule was to be followed. But then: what do I know?

Now five of us struggled back along the beach directly into the teeth of an increasingly cruel and bitter December wind. Conditions continued to worsen and ice pellets began assaulting our faces. The stony beach glistened and crunched under our feet and even the most sure-footed of us were stumbling about like drunkards. My thoughts wandered to my fiancée. (First marriage at the age of forty-eight *and* my first wilderness hike. Best not to read too much into that.) She was expecting me home for a romantic supper. It would have to be a late one.

We stopped just long enough to pull an extra layer from our day packs. Hats were pulled down over ears and waterproof outer shells were tightly zipped over fleece. We hurriedly resumed our retreat to the sheltered cove.

As we straggled into Refugee Cove, it became apparent that much of the valley had been lost to the tide. Gone was the pretty cobblestone beach where we had sat sharing lunch. Gone too was the pleasant microclimate. Icy wind and snow now swept the shrinking valley. The Bay of Fundy crashed violently against the once-welcoming rocks. I felt as I imagine those dispossessed Acadians for whom Refugee Cove is named must have felt, taking refuge here from the British during the "Grand Derangement." *Misérable.* But there was little time to dwell on our predicament.

After a few welcome minutes rest, we ascended the steep escarpment back into the woods.

"Let's go," Dave shouted with an air of authority that precluded any discussion as to why he was now in charge.

Joel's pace had slowed and he seemed to be disassociating himself from our worsening situation. Perhaps he was wishing he had bolted down the beach with Sid. Or perhaps he was cursing the tides. He just seemed to lose interest.

"Buffoonery, pal, sheer buffoonery," he chirped as I climbed past him.

It was already dusk as we re-entered the trail, and the canopy blocked much of the remaining daylight. With a sense of urgency, we picked up our pace. But staying on the trail was frustratingly difficult in the waning light and swirling snow. Nothing looked familiar. We lost and re-found the trail numerous times.

Quicker than anyone had anticipated, we were in complete darkness. I dug in my pockets and was relieved to find my Bic lighter. I was amazed at how little light it threw, how many times it blew out, and how often I burned my thumb getting it lit again. It was next to useless, but it was all we had. Occasionally, we spotted lights out on the bay and we used them to keep the water on our right as we pushed ahead.

Stopping only long enough to pull on a pair of dry socks, I did my duty and examined every tree along our wretched path for an elusive red trail marker. For hours, Dave managed to keep us more or less on track despite the deteriorating conditions.

Then we came to a fork in the road.

The trail splintered.

It was dark.

We thought we could make out signs of a footpath leading down toward the bay and of another that seemed to continue along the current path. Without a marker it was anyone's guess. We split up to look for signs of our trail. As usual, I took the low road.

"Dave, I think I see a marker down here to the right," I yelled kicking through ankle-high snow in a depression that may have been a trail. But in the swirling snow, I couldn't be sure.

"No, pal, I have our trail over here!" Dave hollered, barely audible over the screaming wind. I doubled back, struggling up a steep grade, and reached Dave who was taking shelter under a wind-ravaged spruce. (Okay, it could just as easily been a pine. What do I know?) Dave pointed at a spot on the tree. A flick of my Bic revealed a red marker. Dave had re-found our "well-marked" trail again for the third or fourth time in the space of just a couple of hours.

"Good going, Hawkeye!" I cried, throwing Dave a well-deserved bouquet.

It was now just follow the yellow brick road and on until morning—and I'm pretty sure it was a spruce.

Minutes, then hours, passed. Our pace slackened as we struggled along. I tried to reach Sid on my cellphone. I was sure "the middle of nowhere" was covered by my plan, but apparently not. There was nothing to do but soldier on.

Now, two hours since last seeing a red trail marker, hope was flagging. We needed to get out of these damn woods, and fast.

"Aye, we gotta bushwhack our way out, I tell ye!" spat Sandy for the third time as he stomped away from Joel in a lather. Suddenly he stopped and began taking off his parka. I could sense he was no longer angry. He was concerned.

Then I noticed Claire. She had moved off the trail to my right and had begun to shiver uncontrollably. Her athletic physique did not have the warming layer of body fat mine enjoyed.

"Would ye like my parka, lassie?" Sandy asked gently, wrapping it around her. This time, I was positive he had said "lassie".

"No, I'm all right," Claire answered, as she disappeared inside his oversized parka.

Sandy was one of the good guys after all.

We all huddled around Claire to share our warmth and she recovered quickly.

"Do you think we'll find our way out tonight?" she asked with a slightly wicked smile, clearly enjoying the attention. There it was. The question had been asked. Would we be spending the night in the forest? The inescapable answer was yes. Yes, we would need to stick together and survive the night in this bitter cold—with nary a Tim's in sight.

"We'll need to make a fire, first thing," said Dave, the natural leader. "And let's start gathering up some boughs to make a lean-to."

The four of them burst into action. No panic, just total efficiency. Another day at the office.

"I think these'll do nicely," Sandy said, pulling some broken boughs from under a giant spruce. It may have been a pine. Sandy actually seemed to be enjoying himself, as did the others.

"Gather twigs for kindling and as much treefall as you can find. The fire is number one. Let's get it going. Now!" Dave yelled, shocking me into action. Then he went over to help Sandy build a shelter.

"Steve, bring your Bic over here and we'll get the fire started," hollered Claire, who had hollowed out a hole in the snow and was rimming it with rocks from the path. I stared at her in disbelief. Wasn't she just on the verge of hypothermia?

I handed her my lighter and went to gather more twigs. I felt dizzy. This was special. These people were special. We were going to survive a night in one of the most inhospitable spits of land in Nova Scotia. I was sure of it.

"We're having fun now aren't we, pal?" said Joel, walking up behind me and dumping a load of wood beside the emerging fire pit. The challenge had finally shaken my friend from his lethargy. He seemed totally at ease and even a bit bemused.

"Stick with me, pal!" he intoned as he went to inspect the developing shelter.

Then without warning, apparently satisfied that our preparations were moving apace, he started down the trail.

"Joel, where are you going?" I yelled after him.

"Keep working, pal, it's good practice," he yelled back as he effortlessly negotiated the barely visible trail and disappeared from view.

None of the others seemed the least bit surprised by Joel's unusual behaviour.

"What's he up to?" I asked them.

"You'll see," answered Dave. They continued to build a shelter, working a little less feverishly than before.

As I trudged over to help Claire build a fire, I could hear Sandy and Dave sharing a joke and laughing conspiratorially.

What's got into them? I wondered. Had I missed a memo? Our situation, though somewhat under control, was still less than ideal. It was getting increasingly cold and windy and snow was accumulating quickly. It was going to be a long, difficult night.

Claire flicked the lighter furiously as I added small twigs. An incipient flame was just on the horizon when an apparition appeared from a black hole in the woods.

"Get your things together. We're getting out of here." It was Joel. "Nice work on the fire. Follow me," he ordered.

I was oddly disappointed that our sleepover was so unceremoniously cancelled but we all swiftly grabbed our packs and were again swallowed by the forest.

"Typical Joel Feinstein Adventure," Dave whispered.

"Aye, he doesn't disappoint," Sandy agreed.

"Are we getting lost again?" Claire asked me.

I was still coming up with a witty yet reassuring response when we spilled out onto a wide trail that intersected our narrow path. But it wasn't a trail—it was a road, an old logging road, and it was bathed in moonlight.

"We're not lost. We're just not where we're supposed to be," Joel explained. "Just a forty-five minute's hike down this logging road and we're back at Red Rocks."

"When you say 'down,' do you mean down-left, or down-right?" I asked.

"South," responded Joel, not really answering my question.

I could not image how, but Joel had calculated our bearings in his head and set a true course for home.

I was still dubious and our redemptive moment was further clouded by the fact that Sid was not with us. I tried my cellphone again and this time miraculously got a signal. I immediately dialled his number and received no answer. I tried his home number to see if he had contacted his family. This had to be done delicately to keep from terrifying his wife and kids.

"No, no, we were just checking to see if his cellphone had a signal. Go back to sleep. Nothing to worry about."

But we were worried and finally Joel dialled 911.

"Hello? We'd like to report a missing person in the Cape Chignecto Wilderness Park."

"Is this the hiking party that went out early this morning?"

"Yes...a member of our party got separated and—"

"Just a moment, I'm patching you through to Search and Rescue."

A radio signal crackled and a voice, barely audible amid the static, demanded, "Where are you?"

"A logging road. About forty-five minutes northeast of Red Rocks," Joel explained with an air of casual certainty.

How does he know that? I wondered.

"Stay where you are, we're coming to get you." The vaguely familiar voice cracked and then there was silence.

I took the opportunity to call my fiancée so she could stop worrying. My call woke her up. After assuring herself I was in no imminent danger, she told me not to die or she'd kill me and went back to bed. I fell in love all over again.

Then within minutes we heard a rumble and stared in disbelief at a one-ton truck rolling toward us. And there, hanging halfway out of the cab, yelling and waving furiously, was the ever-flamboyant Sid.

He jumped out as the truck was rolling to a stop and ran over to us, kissing and hugging and crying in obvious relief, much to Joel's annoyance.

"We thought we had lost you! There are search parties out all over the Chignecto trail system!"

Apparently, Sid had easily raced the tide back to Red Rocks. When we didn't arrive before dark, he had alerted the RCMP and the local Search and Rescue sprang into action. The reason we weren't found sooner was because we had trekked so far off the trail system.

"We even had the fishing boats out flooding the cliffs with light."

Whoops. I recalled seeing their lights just before we hiked inland and remember fearing they were searching for Sid. I now realized they were looking for us.

Joel continued to protest, insisting we didn't need to be rescued as we piled into the back of the truck. Within forty minutes we were sitting in the Advocate Harbour Fire Hall, which had served as Search and Rescue headquarters. The local auxiliary was pouring us warm drinks and wrapping us in blankets. Cheerful ladies were bringing out overflowing trays of sandwiches and sweets. The search parties, fresh off the trail, began to trickle in and helped themselves to some well-earned refreshment as they rolled out maps and explained where we had gone wrong. Turns out Joel had it exactly right: we had trekked inland on an abandoned trail clear out of the wilderness park to a logging road northeast of Red Rocks.

As for our rescuers, there was no reproach, no complaint. They had merely done what neighbours do in a small coastal town. They had unhesitatingly interrupted their own lives to bring a lost party to safety and we were grateful and extremely humbled. They even seemed surprised when we passed a hat to give them a wholly insufficient reward. It was not about the money but they would accept it. The fire hall was in need of a new bathroom and the roof was a bit iffy. It would be put to good use. I learned a lot.

There would be time to examine what went wrong. Why had we gone so miserably off course? Where was the flashlight? Why were there identical red markers on two, very different trails? Why had the group separated against well-established practice? How had we got the tides wrong? What was the advisability of planning a trek in the middle of December in the first place?

Joel would convene an informal enquiry at Sid's oceanside house where these questions and many others would be totally vetted over a sip of rum. He would also demand and receive an apology from the *Halifax Daily Journal* for misreporting the tides charts.

But that was for later. For now, sitting wrapped in a warm blanket and listening to the excited chatter that filled the fire hall, it was enough to reflect upon the day and what was truly, "A most excellent adventure."

THE NIGHT OF THE POPCORN PENALTY

Norma Jean MacPhee

*I*t hits as you walk through the doorway. Energy. Fervor. Anticipation. Bodies jostle in the main foyer as people hand over their tickets. Buoyant ushers in Cape Breton tartan skirts greet the fans, rip their tickets in half, and wish them a good game.

It's a cold Friday night at Centre 200 in February 1993. Cape Breton Oilers versus Halifax Citadels.

American rock band Survivor blasts through the building as the teams whip around the ice warming up.

Throngs of people weave through the crowd. Some lean casually against the rail of the lower bowl watching the players. Others head directly for the even split table.

"I only want the winning ticket," each and every person says to the fella who hands out the square orange tickets.

Young people circle the perimeter of the rink, checking for their latest flame.

"O Canada" finishes and before long players are in place for the game's first faceoff.

Thunk.

Twack.

Thud.

The puck boomerangs around the rink from sticks like the silver game piece in a pinball machine. Bells and whistles erupt when the

Oilers succeed in getting the puck past the goalie's pads. Young boys and girls haul crates of chocolate bars, chips, and popcorn up and down the numbered metal stairs. Section to section, their weary feet grow ever slower with each passing period.

Hecklers voice their expert opinions with booming voices.

"Need my glasses, ref?"

"Ahh, what a pretty little dive."

"The net! It's the net you're looking for!"

"Oh, do you want my purse to go along with your dress?" when a fisticuff takes on more of a ballroom rhythm than the desired rock 'em, sock 'em two-step.

Amidst these vocal fans there are the regulars—those who cheer when goals are scored, clap when the goalie makes a neat glove save, and enjoy a good slam of the opponents against the boards.

One such woman rarely misses a game. Maria sits directly behind the visitor's bench. Her seat offers an intimate glimpse of the players as they shuffle along between shifts on the ice. Not only is it directly behind the bench, but it is also the last seat in the row, which allows her to see clearly into the area where the players enter and leave the dressing rooms. In that same alcove sits the back-up goalie in full gear, awaiting his big break. Spare sticks blaring the name of each player stand by for duty. A trainer also hovers in the area, busy replacing broken sticks and handing out fresh ones as needed. The seats are perfectly situated for fans to ask players for a coveted stick at the end of a game. An outstretched hand easily fits between the white cement railings. Not that Maria ever asked for sticks, of course, but her eager niece and other young children took advantage of the opportunity whenever they could.

Through the thick Plexiglas Maria watches the coach chomp his gum. They must all be required to swear a stone-faced oath before they are handed their clipboard and title, she thinks. Never do the curves of their lips take any shape other than a straight line. The players' lips move, however—colourful expletives spurt from their mouths when things aren't going so well.

Like tonight. Amidst a flurry of shaven ice, a frustrated player, just shut down by the Oilers's goalie, stops in front of the door to the bench.

"Fuck," he mutters and the door automatically opens.

"Must be the secret password," Jessie says to her old friend Maria.

"Haha! Not so secret, though," Maria manages to croak out between gasps for air.

Maria and Jessie have been coming to games ever since the team arrived in Sydney several years earlier. Both season ticket holders, Jessie has two seats in another section. More often than not, Maria's husband opts to watch the game from one of the private boxes up above. It's from this vantage point he witnesses—quite helplessly—his wife nearly get thrown out of the game.

BUZZ.

The second period comes to an end all tied up at 2–2. The Halifax players swish by Maria as they quickly shuffle from their bench and head back to their dressing room.

"I'm going to grab some even splits," Jessie says to Maria.

"Well, I may as well go for the walk myself," Maria replies.

Off they go and join the fray of intermission.

"Well, hello there."

Sydney being what it is, Maria and Jessie are collectively related to half the island; they barely get halfway up the section before they stop to talk.

In this start-stop fashion, they make their way to the main concourse, buy their tickets and snacks, and eventually wend their way back to their seats. Maria balances a bag of popcorn on her lap. Jessie opted for a chocolate bar.

Players on the bench bang their sticks in anticipation of the third period. They want to win. With the two teams in the same province, it notches up the rivalry meter for the players. And for the fans.

We all know hockey fans—they are a different breed. As for the Cape Breton Oilers fans, the players are almost family extensions. This year the team is top of their division. The Calder Cup looms more and more like a tangible possibility. Perhaps this explains what happened next.

Some nights are scrappier than others. This particular evening was one of those nights. The ref's lips grow tired from blowing his whistle and the linesmen receive their share of elbows and punches as they attempt to pry players apart.

There is only 7:34 remaining: "Francois to Haas. He's in the crease now. He shoots—he SCORES!"

The Oilers fans erupt. Trumpets blare, horns honk, and hands are sore from clapping.

The tension increases. The Halifax players turn to every defensive move, those on the books and off. The intensity wafts from the ice to the stands and back. The crescendo of yells in the stands magnifies with each penalty assigned.

"Get off the island—you're not welcome here!" a woman's voice cuts through the clatter.

Number 22 of the Citadels has been dogging the Oilers's forwards all night long. A sneaky poke of the stick here, a from-behind smack into the boards there.

"Boooo! Get him out of there, ref!" Maria shouts.

Now it's important here to tell you a little about Maria: a demure, holy woman, she leads prayer sessions and counsels people in spiritual guidance. Her long dark hair flows in gentle waves around her kind, soothing face. While she loves a good laugh (which is what she regularly receives in Jessie's company), she also can seriously discuss and advise on difficult personal issues.

Now there is just 4:57 remaining on the clock. The Oilers lead 3–2. The Citadels are gunning for it, attacking for the puck and scrapping at every chance. Number 22 continues to thwack all the players, particularly Cape Breton's power line.

The puck drops deep in the Oilers zone. They win control. Van Allen skirts it to Currie. Currie carries it forward without hesitation. A hush covers the stands. All that can be heard is the *swush-swush* of his sharp blades. He has a clear breakaway.

Then a flash of blue flies from the Citadels's bench—number 22. With a deft hook and crosscheck, Currie collapses to the ice.

Centre 200 bursts with screams and stomps, Maria chief among them. A whistle blows and the ref and linesmen confer. Currie struggles to his feet and winces as he skates back to his bench. The booing continues. Everyone is on their feet.

Finally a linesman leads number 22 not to the penalty box, but back to his bench. Game misconduct—the player is ejected. He opens the heavy door and bangs it closed. Number 22 doesn't look at his team's bench, but heads directly for the dressing room, head down.

Jessie watches with everyone else as the thug finally leaves the game. Maria's husband watches from above where he sits with the Oilers's general manager. But Maria is no longer just watching. In a genuine reflex, she lifts her half-full bag of popcorn and dumps it on number 22's head as he passes.

"You saucy, dirty, little pup," she yells as she shakes out the last kernels.

Shock stops him in his tracks. He shoots Maria an angry look, doesn't say a word, and keeps walking. His blades *crunch, crunch* through the little buttered pieces.

Maria sits back down. Jessie—along with the entire Citadels team—stares at her in disbelief. Her husband is already in the elevator on his way to her, assuming he'll have to explain something to the security officials.

"Now that he's taken care of, we can finish this game in peace," Maria says.

CONNOR AND THE SNOW COAT
Steve Vernon

My grandfather Hanlan loved to sit by the crackling fireplace and spin out yarns so long you could have knit a five-mile-long scarf and still have yarn left over for mittens and a matching toque. The funny thing was, each story started out the same way: "One time it…"

It was almost like if he did not use those three words, the story wasn't ever going to get itself told.

"One time it snowed so hard the eye doctor had to start handing out ice scrapers with every pair of glasses he sold," he told me once. "It was colder than a polar bear's pajamas. We couldn't even tell what temperature it was because the mercury in the thermometer was so scared of the cold it wouldn't come up high enough for us to see it. There was so much salt sprinkled on the roads a fellow could grow himself a case of high blood pressure just trying to cross the road. We had to string ropes between ourselves so we would not get lost, only then the rope froze into icicles and we slid into each other and created the world's largest parka lot traffic jam."

I am not really sure just why my grandfather used to talk so very much about the weather, but then again we lived in an awfully small town called Lunenburg, Nova Scotia. What passed for lively conversation here usually ran somewhere in the vicinity of "Well, the tide went out this morning. I expect it'll be back in for afternoon tea."

Well, let me tell you a story about a boy named Connor.

The weatherman had promised snow that day. Connor had heard him promise it on the television set.

Connor dreamed of snow all night long. He dreamed of waking up and seeing snowbanks higher than the roof of his school—and if you have ever seen just exactly how high the top of the Lunenburg schoolhouse is, way up on top of Gallows Hill, then you know very well that we are talking snowbanks deep enough to bog down jet planes.

Well, the morning came just like mornings always do and Connor slid sock footed from his bedroom down the freshly waxed hall to the big bay window.

There was absolutely nothing outside. No more than a handful of dried-up pitiful little flakes. The plowmen didn't start up the big snow plow. The street cleaners came out of winter retirement and cleaned the street with dainty silver teaspoons and salted it down with a tiny glass saltshaker one of them had borrowed from their Aunt Myrtle. Connor stared out the window like it was a television set with nothing on it but reruns of last year's midtown dart tournament.

School would not be closed.

"The weatherman lied," Connor complained to his mother. "He said there would be heaps and heaps of snow."

"The weatherman doesn't control the weather," Connor's mother answered. "That is the job of Old Man Winter."

"Well I would like to kick Old Man Winter in his big snowy butt."

"That's not a very nice thing to say."

"I have to say something, don't I?" Connor asked his mother. "Just where exactly does Old Man Winter live?"

"Why don't you go and ask your grandfather? He knows a lot more about winter than I do—but you had better ask him on your way to school. And be quick about it," Connor's mother said, using that special tone of ice-cold voice mothers always save for children running late for school or failing to do their weekend chores.

Connor ran to his grandfather's big shiny silver trailer, which was painted a candy cane pink and green and squatted halfway down the road between Connor's home and his school.

Grandfather stood in the backyard, talking softly to a big old blue jay.

"I have no peanuts for you, mister blue jay," Grandfather said. "I am far too busy today. The wind needs pointing in the proper direction to blow and the smaller birds require singing lessons. Then there are those last few stubborn leaves that must be encouraged to let go of their trees and jump for it, parachutes or not."

The blue jay knew better. He landed on the old man's shoulder and he daintily dipped his big old beak into grandfather's many-pocketed vest.

Grandfather's vest had hundreds of pockets, sewn one atop the other. Any time he wanted, he could reach down into a pocket and pull out a jackknife or a piece of string or a pack of chewing gum or a can opener or even a peanut. One Christmas morning he even pulled an entire electric train set from one of his pockets. No one quite knows how he did that, but he did—because Connor saw him.

"You are wearing your face longer than stretched-out well rope," Grandfather said to Connor. "Just why exactly are you so very glum today?"

"It is Old Man Winter's fault," Connor said. "He did not send us down enough snow. I wanted to stay at home and to watch cartoons on television, and now I have to go to school and study, which sucks harder than an anteater with a corked-up snout."

Grandfather laughed so hard his grey whiskers rattled like a line full of frozen clothespins. "Cartoons are flat. The world is round," he said. "You would be better off if you could get your head out of the television set and down into your school work. Read a book and grow your mind a little."

Grandfather always talked like that. Connor loved him and all, but the bone-hard fact of it was Grandfather was so darned old-fashioned he honestly believed websites were nothing more than the places crawly spiders built their fuzz-nests.

"So just where exactly does Old Man Winter live, Grandfather?"

"Farther north than the polar bear. Farther north than the Inuit.

Farther north than the snow geese fly. Farther north than north can go, that is where Old Man Winter hangs his snow coat."

"Can you walk there?"

"You would need a pair of snowshoes and a good strong set of legs. Now hurry up and get yourself to school."

Connor dreamed of snow all morning long.

When his math teacher asked him what two plus two equalled, Connor just said, "snow."

When his French teacher asked him if he could *"parlez vous?"* Connor said, "snow."

When the school nurse asked him if he felt okay, he just said, "snow." Only the nurse thought Connor had said "no," so she sent him home.

Connor came back home and he let himself in with his key.

His mother worked all day and his father had gone off a long time ago and never bothered coming back. So Connor was all alone. He watched television for a while, but then he felt just a little bit guilty for being home without a good reason. He tried to play with the cat but she only wanted to nap. He lay on his bed and he counted dust dancers as they twinkled down from his ceiling lamp.

Only that didn't help either.

The drifting dust dancers just reminded him of snowflakes falling down from cotton-batten clouds, and he got sadder and madder until he felt like he was going to burst.

"That darned Old Man Winter," Connor muttered out loud. "This is all his fault."

Then he got himself an idea.

It wasn't just any ordinary sort of idea, you understand. This was the sort of idea that could shake an entire civilization down into anthills.

"A pair of snowshoes and a good strong set of legs," Connor said, thinking about what his grandfather had told him.

Connor dressed in his warmest winter gear. He duct taped badminton rackets to his boots because grandfather said that he would need snowshoes. He packed a can of tomato soup and a carton of crunchy crisp crackers into his pillowcase. He duct taped the pillowcase around his parka. Then he borrowed his mother's broom for a walking stick. He didn't think she would really mind. After all, she hated sweeping more than birds hated cats.

Then he started to walk, following the flight of the snow geese.

"Farther north than north can go is where I want to be," Connor said to himself.

It was an awfully long walk from Lunenburg, Nova Scotia, to Old Man Winter's home. Of course, it would have been a whole lot longer if Connor had lived in Florida so he told himself he ought not complain.

"It is better to be glad about one tiny little thing than miserable about everything that you can think of," Connor told himself.

He whistled for company.

When his whistle froze in mid-air, Connor knew he must be getting close. Since his mouth was no longer full of whistle, Connor felt a little bit hungry. He opened up the pillowcase for the can of tomato soup, only to realize he had forgotten to bring along a can opener.

"The carton of crunchy crisp crackers will have to do," he told himself. He munched away happily.

Awoken by the crunching, a great big white polar bear jumped out of a snowdrift and growled. It was either a gee-I'm-happy-to-see-you growl or a let-me-get-ready-to-eat-you growl.

Connor acted fast.

He reached into the pillowcase and he pulled out the unopened tin of tomato soup. He threw it with all his might. The bear caught the soup tin in its teeth, crushed down, and sucked the tomato soup with a loud bottom-of-the-milkshake slurping sound. The soup tasted so darned good that the big old bear lay down for a little nap.

Connor tiptoed quietly past the sleeping polar bear.

Connor, his pillowcase lightened by both soup can and crackers, made better time until the blizzard began to blow. The wind howled hard and snow stuck to his parka. He looked a lot like a boy-sized snowball on two legs. There was nothing but his knitted hat and broomstick showing. When he stomped past an Inuit village the Inuit thought he was some kind of a big terrible snowman. They ran away.

"I have gone farther than the polar bear and I have gone farther than the Inuit," Connor said. "I must really be getting close to where Old Man Winter hangs his snow coat."

When Connor saw the snow geese turning back in their flight, he knew that he was almost there. Connor walked until the world was made of nothing but snow. Snow blew all around and it covered up his footsteps before he even made them. He was farther north than north could go.

"This is the Snow Country," Connor decided. "There is no other name for it."

In the centre of a great white field stood a coat tree made of hard frozen icicles. Hanging from this coat tree was a long white coat. From out of the coat's inner lining a howling blizzard blew.

"This must be Old Man Winter's snow coat," Connor marvelled. "If I borrow it, I can have snow whenever I want to."

Connor thought about that for a minute.

He thought about having snow days all winter long and staying home and watching all of the television he ever wanted to watch. He thought that would be a pretty good thing. So he folded the coat up and carried it back home—which was an AWFULLY long way to carry a coat full of snow.

Connor tiptoed around the village so as not to scare the Inuit again.

The polar bear woke from his nap. It growled at Connor and it might have eaten him up, but Connor opened the snow coat wide and the built-up blizzard blasted the bear clear into Hudson Bay. The last Connor saw of that bear was its big white bear butt poking out above the waves while the bear frantically paddled for shore.

Connor walked until his badminton racket snowshoes wore down to ping pong paddles. When he finally got home, Grandfather was standing and waiting in his yard outside of his big shiny silver trailer, like he had been waiting there all along.

"I have been to visit the snow country," Connor told him.

"I know you have," Grandfather said. "I can see that by the snow still hanging off of you."

Then he took the snow coat from Connor.

"Thank you very much for bringing me my snow coat. You saved an old man a considerably long walk."

And for the very first time, Connor noticed just how crisp and snowy-white Grandfather's whiskers and eyebrows were. His eyes twinkled like the ice dancing across flat frozen fields.

"Grandfather!" Connor said in shock and surprise. "You have never *ever* told me that you were really Old Man Winter."

"You have never asked me," Grandfather said with a mischievous wink. "But if I remember correctly, you *did* ask for snow."

Grandfather shook the snow coat so hard snow covered the rooftops of Lunenburg.

"Is that enough snow for you?" Grandfather Winter asked.

Connor shook his head. "Nope. There needs to be more."

Grandfather Winter shook the coat until snow covered all the treetops on the surrounding hillsides.

"Is that enough snow for you?"

"No," Connor said. "I walked way too far. I need more snow than that."

So Grandfather Winter shook and shook and *shook* out that big old snow coat until the snow had covered the highest hill in town and you could see the black-painted windows of the Lunenburg Academy.

"Now *that* is enough snow for me," Connor said.

"Good," said Grandfather Winter. "Because that is all that you are getting for this year."

Then he folded the snow coat up and he tucked it down into his deepest vest pocket and he walked away to talk to the blue jay who was considerably confused by the sudden depth of snow.

There was so much snow on the ground that winter school was closed until June. But to make up for all the lost lessons, the principal and teachers decided school would need to stay open all summer long.

And Connor never wished for snow again.

OVERNIGHT AT MASON'S CABIN
Paul Skerry

In the beginning, it was just a winter Saturday afternoon like any other. It began with staggering out of bed and greeting the day at about noon, wolfing down a high-cholesterol brunch, and then scratching around for something to do for the bulk of the weekend.

We were all young then—it was the late 1970s—and we were of that generation fully convinced we would be young forever; invincible enough to handle anything Nova Scotia could hand out in the way of a challenge. It was standard practice to fling ourselves off into the wilds and come out grinning, sometimes a little wet and chilled, but nothing a bottle of rum couldn't solve. Summer or winter, no difference; the challenge was just a matter of different clothes and equipment, along with a determination not to whine.

I decided to visit my old friend Jack, who I knew from engineering school at Dalhousie. Since we both elected to stay in Nova Scotia to develop our careers, we had fostered an intermittent friendship based on our love of the outdoors and acts of physical bravado—although Jack was a lot more accomplished than me; I was just a weekend warrior.

Jack was a man's man: the right size, strong, and well muscled, educated (at least as far as could be achieved locally), smiling personality, and a natural athletic ability. Jack could always be depended on to come up with some hare-brained idea for a trip, somewhat like Burt Reynolds in the movie *Deliverance*. Later in life, that movie chilled us all with its similarity to our trips and the lead into the well-known chain of events that made it famous (except one, thank God). However, we managed to never kill, lose, or cause anybody serious harm—at least not yet! Like I said, though, we were still young and trying.

This particular Saturday was a lovely sunny afternoon in February with lots of snow on the ground—just the type of day to foster some idea of a ski trip into the wilds. Although it was really too late in the day to organize a trip, Jack and I did not let that daunt us, and quickly hatched a plan to ski to Mason's Cabin, which was located deep in the wilderness on the boundary of Kejimkujik National Park and the Tobeatic Wilderness Reserve. I claimed the cabin was there, having located and used it as a refuge during a canoe trip to retrace the famous tent dwellers trip the year of my graduation. *The Tent Dwellers* if you ever read it, is a good yarn and took place in that part of the country at the turn of the twentieth century. That location is about as far away from anywhere as you could get in Nova Scotia. And it was this, in our naiveté, which appealed to us most.

Without much more thought or attempt at organization, we gathered our skis and gear and sallied forth with our usual enthusiasm. In those days, it was wooden skis, bamboo poles, three-toe pin ski boots, Swix wax, wool toques, army sleeping bags, and various other pieces of gear gleaned from the local army-navy surplus store. It wasn't good equipment, but we were planning to spend the night in a cabin, and the cabin had a wood stove that the National Park serviced and stocked with firewood. We only had to get ourselves there! It would be grand! The thirty-kilometre distance to the cabin seemed to be just an abstract number.

We arrived at Keji just in time to see the sun set. For most explorers that would have been cause for hesitation, but it was not enough to deter us. We were dancing about like a bunch of hunting dogs, dying to get going. We started off trailing half of our hastily prepared gear behind us as we flew down the first section of trail, hardly looking back to make sure the car doors were closed.

That first section of trail takes you from the old fish hatchery at Grafton Lake to George's Landing, where the Mersey River exits from George Lake—about eight kilometres. The first incline increased my heartbeat to a thundering roar, and got the blood moving in such a way that the plunging temperatures seemed to be the last of my concerns. All was excitement and power. The open trail beckoned! That section winds its way through undulating terrain past the Peter Point turnoff and onto the Mersey River. We fairly flew that first section of the trip in the gathering darkness.

Jack was the stronger skier and it wasn't long before I was left to my own devices, puffing up hills and gliding down inclines, trying to find the right wax for the conditions. I had always loved the forest, and particularly enjoyed the tranquility of that first section of trail. When I finally arrived at the bridge crossing the Mersey River, I found Jack waiting for me on the riverbank. We stopped for a break and a drink, and replenished our water bottles in the river.

The river was open except for a rim of ice along the shore, and the dark waters were quietly flowing past our vantage point, as it does summer and winter. During the fishing season this was a favourite spot for anglers to test their luck with the local trout population— even I had a few riverside memories. After my graduation in 1971 I had spent a couple of weeks on a canoe trip doing the Kejimkujik lakes—the Shelburne River, Lake Rossignol, and Mersey River loop—with a classmate, Larry Olsheski. We had spent one night camping just opposite the riverbank near what had once been once a forest lodge. The lodge was long gone, even at that time, except for the column of the surviving stone fireplace and chimney.

It was Parks Canada policy to destroy all existing lodges when they converted the area into a national park. Soon after our trip they tightened their administrative grip on the area again, with their enforced policy of allowing camping in designated spots only.

The black water of the river tumbled past like time itself, taking with it all the mysteries and memories of life.

The next section of the trail starts with a short sharp incline and runs for six kilometres to the base of Peskowesk Lake—our next planned stop. Crossing the bridge over the Mersey, being careful not to break a ski pole in the open grid, we flung ourselves into the steep first climb and then established the rhythm for the next section of the journey. By now it was completely dark, the residual light of the sunset having faded away, but the moon's reflecting off the snow and the openness of the forest canopy still allowed for good visibility.

We arrived at the base of Peskowesk Lake, and the winter camping site there, in great spirits, full of exuberance. We had a bit of a lark there racing around and tumbling in the snow and generally making fools of ourselves. This we paid dearly for later as our snow-encrusted wool clothes rained melting snow from our necks and wrists onto our now-chilled bodies.

Up until this point other skiers had already broken the trail and we had a relatively easy time of it. Leaving Peskowesk Lake for the next leg of the journey (thirteen kilometres), we rounded a corner and found ourselves breaking trail in a couple feet of soft powder. This was another kettle of fish altogether, and our progress dropped from an easy glide to a difficult slog. The effort went up and the speed went down, and so did the temperature.

Had we known then what was in store, we would have turned around and skied right back to our vehicle. But such is the optimism of youth: abandoning the trip never crossed our minds.

This next section of the trail parallels the shoreline of Peskowesk Lake, and the terrain is mostly open hardwood forest with good visibility and relatively flat. At times like that, when it's just one foot in front of the other, the mind tends to wander. My memories took me back to June 1971, when Larry and I walked this very section of trail in our rubber boots, trying to keep ahead of the swarming mosquitoes as we did our forced march for the much-needed supplies cached at George Lake. Then, as now, the trail seemed to go on forever.

The temperature was really plummeting now. Despite the effort of skiing, the cold was becoming brutal. The snow was up to our knees and too soft to offer any support, so we were pushing snow and pumping our legs with little or no glide. The only good thing was snow conditions were constant so there was no need to stop and reapply wax for changing conditions.

When we left the base of Peskowesk Lake, a full moon rose into a spectacular star-filled sky. The moonlight flooded the forest with an intense low-angle light that generated the most beautiful designs. The snow sparkled like diamonds, and the trees cast long black shadows across its undulating surface, making intricate patterns and contrasts. The wind was gone completely and the silence of the wilderness was profound. I will never forget that night—it was one of the most beautiful things I have ever experienced. When I shut my eyes today, I can still imagine it like it was yesterday.

Jack was much stronger and had surged ahead breaking trail, leaving me to my thoughts. It was so quiet it seemed like I could hear the blood coursing through my head, and certainly I could feel my heart pounding with the workout. Suddenly, I was startled by a deep and soft escalation of breath. Because of the proximity of the sound, the hair on the back of my neck rose. It's funny how quickly you tumble out of the embrace of reason and you are seized by the primeval grasp of fear when surrounded by a dark wilderness.

The moon was higher now, and its light was shining down in a more direct angle, clearly illuminating everything around me. I could see some distance into the forest, but nothing stirred—at least nothing mortal that could breathe a sigh like the one I had just heard. I paused, studying my surroundings more intensely.

I couldn't see anything to account for the sound—only the silence of the woods punctuated by the pounding of my heart. I had clearly heard a deep exhalation of what seemed like a breath, followed by a distinct sigh. Were my senses playing games with me? This was an ancient Mi'kmaw burial site; could it be the spirit of a long-dead chief, or a manifestation of some mysterious winter spirit?

Uneasy and still unable to account for the sound, I started skiing again, instinctively wanting to get away from the spot and its mysterious threats, and catch up with Jack. I shuffled along and suddenly the sound happened again. This time I was more alert, and I stopped skiing as if I had been shot.

I was in a clearing and the wind-sculpted snow was unblemished in every direction. I studied the snow intensely for a clue, and *there!* On the other side of the clearing came a sigh. Suddenly I understood. The snow had piled up a number of feet and the underlying snow had subsided, leaving a dome-like structure. When I skied by, I had created a disturbance, causing it to collapse and release a puff of air and a deep sigh like a creature's. It probably would have gone unnoticed but for the extreme silence of the night. I had never experienced this peculiar phenomenon before, or since!

As the night wore on, I made progress down the length of Peskowesk Lake and found Jack waiting for me beside the trail near the headwaters of Beaverskin Lake. The cold was intense and when we stopped, the icy chill seemed like daggers stabbing through our clothes. We couldn't stop for long, just long enough for a quick energy snack of chocolate. I remember the chocolate shattering like glass—we shared the shards, melting them in our mouths. My sense of taste was acute because of the cold, and I remember the intense taste of chocolate. We found out later that this was one of the coldest nights of that winter, reaching minus twenty-eight. All we knew at the time was that it was really cold; we didn't need a thermometer for that.

After our snack, the next section of trail took us into a deep evergreen forest of pine and spruce with a canopy that made it very dim. To make matters worse, the moon had now set below the horizon and we were really in complete darkness now. We were well into the night—it was probably around 3:00 A.M.—and the terrain had become undulating, with sharp steep inclines and corresponding declines. Skiing these downhill sections was somewhat of a challenge because you couldn't see anything. It required a lot of faith that the trail wouldn't take a sudden turn at the bottom, just when our speed was the greatest.

Jack had the advantage of breaking trail, his velocity moderated by the snow. I had some very exciting descents, flailing around with my poles, trying to maintain my balance while searching for some visual clue in the blackness to give me guidance, expecting at any moment to be knocked into the trees. Sometimes I was and quickly executed a face plant, which didn't help with the imminent threat of freezing to death. You would be surprised by how intensely you can concentrate when a failure in stability might result in a deep-snow face plant.

We were getting really tired, and Jack kept asking me how much further to the cabin. The answer was, I really didn't know. I was just going by memory and I had been in this neck of the woods only once before. We had a number of navigation stops with a flashlight to consult our schematic map to do some estimates, but in the end we became very discouraged and unsure of our location. The trail just seemed to keep going, and the snow remained featureless, indicating that nobody had been there all winter. Had the cabin been demolished like all the others in the park? And had we passed the spot where it used to be and were circumnavigating the park boundaries? Surely we would have seen something. Perhaps we had missed a turn in the trail and were on our way to Poison Ivy Falls.

Uncertainty and fatigue eventually became unbearable, and we start considering stopping for the night to bivouac in the woods. I was spent. I sat down on a rock to consider our limited options. Jack was nervous about resting too long in the intense cold, so he pressed on down the trail.

Just when things seemed the bleakest, I heard Jack shout. He had found the cabin!

I was on my feet in a flash, and only a hundred feet or so further down the trail, there was the cabin. Covered in snow, it had obviously been undisturbed since the start of the winter. I had read many stories of expeditions perishing literally within sight of safety.

Add to that, another.

Forcing the door open, we entered the frozen cabin. It was in good order, but gripped in a vicelike freeze. The windows were frosted with a deep coating of ice, and all material within the cabin were many degrees below freezing. The wood stove was an old Lunenburg Foundry flat top cooking stove (definitely not airtight or efficient by any means) and the walls were not insulated. But to us it looked like a palace!

With some effort we got a fire going. At first, it seemed like the chimney was so cold the smoke refused to go up to create the necessary draft, but in the end we had it glowing with a merry fire, crackling with lifesaving energy. Jack was so cold he put a stool on top of the stove and sat on it to get maximum heat. The cabin didn't seem to warm up appreciatively—everything inside and out was just too cold. It was going to take hours to heat up.

We needed a hot drink and some energy fast, so we tried heating up a pot of soup. I remember spilling some of the liquid during preparation and it froze solid when it hit the floor. It didn't thaw until the next day. It put me in mind of a Jack London story where prospectors in the Yukon would watch the frost crawl across the floor like demonic fingers reaching for flesh. The little bit of heat the stove was generating was having an effect and my feet and fingers, and they began to thaw out. It hurt like hell. Jack said his feet were killing him, and I said not to worry there should be no serious damage unless his flesh was black. He took off his socks and—horror of horrors!—his toes were black. But what could be done now but endure the pain and fondle one's worry beads? The damage was done.

We puttered around for a bit, but fatigue descended like a lead blanket. We unrolled our sleeping bags and laid down, both for the need to rest and to generate some healing warmth in the cocoon of a sleeping bag. I prepared my bed on the top of two wooden benches near the stove, so I could continue to feed it with firewood during the rest of the night without getting out of my bag. As soon as I lay down and felt the first glimmers of warmth, I was dead to the world.

The next thing I knew the sunlight was streaming in through the windows, and it was well into morning of the next day.

The fire had long gone out, but the sunshine made all the difference in the world—it seemed almost civilized in the cabin. My feet were noticeably numb due to nerve damage, and I looked over at Jack to see how he was doing. He was sitting up and said his feet had been bothering him so much during the night that he hadn't slept a wink! We both took off our socks and studied our feet: his, a peculiar black colour, mine, white and colourless. Both pairs a cause for some concern. Why had his feet been more damaged than mine? Well, you could see the reason right away: mine were these little, square, English feet with the toes all squished together; his were more normal-looking, with the toes splayed apart (they looked much nicer but dissipated heat faster). Plus, he had done the lion's share of breaking trail in the deep powder.

I didn't like the look of Jack's feet, and thought he shouldn't be skiing on them anymore. I proposed to ski out and coordinate a rescue with the park warden, but Jack wouldn't hear of it. He wasn't going to be left behind to freeze to death alone in this wilderness cabin. We prepared some more hot drinks and a quick breakfast, and both prepared to ski out. So much for hanging around and enjoying the wilderness, something we had been pining for just yesterday! It was going to be another forced march to get out as fast as possible. (This turned out to be the general pattern for all our trips; there was never any rest or gentle communing with nature.)

We both wore double socks with a plastic bag between the layers to protect our feet from snowmelt water, which would increase the heat loss. It seemed like a good idea at the time, and perhaps it would prevent chafing and irritating the blisters that we had achieved last night. We both emerged in the sunlight and prepped our skis, re-waxing and fine-tuning our preparations.

Mason's cabin is located on a short portage trail connecting Peskawa Lake to Pebbeloggitch Lake and the headwaters of the Shelburne River. It is a beautiful area of undulating terrain, a patchwork of granite-fringed lakes, large pine trees, and sweeping views. The weather was cold but wonderfully clear, and the vista outside the cabin was picture-perfect: the cerulean-blue sky, the dark-green forest, and the intense white of the snow, all enveloped in the silent grip of winter. It seemed like everything was holding its breath. But not so us—we were off on another heart-pounding marathon, back to where we came from, as quickly as possible.

The sunlight on the undulating terrain we had crossed the night previous gave it a whole new aspect, which was much less threatening because you could actually see where you were going. Some of our ski tracks from last night were as straight as an arrow, the pole plants far apart, indicating the unrestrained speed with which we had done the sharp descents. When we reached a spot on the trail where we could see the end of Beaverskin Lake, I found an old woods road that would take us to the Shore of Peskowesk Lake (there had once been a saw mill there). We forged ahead to the lakeshore, intent on shortening the trip by skiing down the lake's surface. That promised to make the return trip quicker.

The wind had scoured and packed snow on top of the lake ice, reducing the effort of skiing and increasing our speed. At one point I looked behind me and noticed water running up my tracks. This fear of crashing through the ice—together with the light tailwind—really helped us cover distance quickly. I remembered from years before a park ranger telling me that the ice on these lakes couldn't be trusted, and there were places in the lakes where the water had a Pollyanna upwelling. The lake would remain open or thinly iced over, and was very dangerous to travel on, even in really cold weather.

We weighed one danger against another—drowning versus freezing to death—and persisted with skiing on the lake ice.

We entered the forest at the end of Peskowesk Lake near the wilderness campground adjacent to the trail we skied the previous night. We rested for a moment, and then retraced our trip from the night before. It looked like we were going to make it. There remained just the section to the Mersey River Bridge at George Lake before the final leg to our vehicle at Grafton Lake. It was a beautiful winter day, just the sort of day we had pined for a mere twenty-four hours before. We beat a hasty retreat and raced back to the vehicle and safety.

In those days I had a Dodge camper van. I had never been so glad to see it sitting at the end of a trail, the ultimate bastion of civilization and comfort. Imagine sitting comfortably on your ass with the heater blasting away, floating over the landscape as if on a magic carpet! What a marvellous invention is a motorized vehicle! There was a panicky yanking on the doors followed by a great clattering of discarded skis as we both sprung into the camper's protective interior. Nothing but deadly silence as we departed the park, heater on max and our vision frozen on to the exit road. If we were lucky we could make the hospital at Bridgewater before the five o'clock shift change, when we hypothesized all the doctors went home for supper.

I'm sure during that silent drive to Bridgewater, Jack was imagining he would have to have his feet amputated. When we got him up on the gurney in the hospital examining room, the doctor took one look and asked him where he lived. Jack nearly fell off in a dead faint. He always was a little squeamish.

In the end, Jack didn't lose his feet, just sustained a lot of tissue damage that took months to rehabilitate…and perhaps a smouldering resentment that I was responsible. As for me, after three months, the nerves in my feet grew back and I could feel them again—not much of an inconvenience.

It was some time before Jack and I planned another trip, and by that time the treat of freezing to death was replaced with the possibility of drowning on a canoe trip. I guess memory has a habit of erasing all the negatives.

Because of the notoriety of our first winter ski trip to Mason's Cabin, it became an annual tradition and proved that we were both capable of comfortably mastering such a challenge. The park service, on my suggestion, installed a new airtight stove and fully insulated the cabin. The very next trip, the following winter, had me standing outside stark naked in a snowdrift in the middle of the night to cool down because the boys had stoked up the wood stove before retiring for the night. That, together with my winter sleeping bag, had put my body temperature near the spontaneous-combustion level. A lesson in extremes.

BOARD ICE
Wayne Curtis

*I*t is a breezy mid-October noon. We have been here since morning. There is a dullness in the air, so I have built a fire to lighten the day. I stand beside the blaze and watch my clients fishing the rapids. There is McGill, Findlay, Scaling, and Taylor. Out in the chest-deep water, they look like busts of the rich and famous that stand in town squares. Between them and me, wedges of granite emerge from the water—the backs of rhinos, oddly shaped pyramids, and miniature castles—draped now with veils of purple seaweed. All the leaves have fallen, and dead rushes stick out of eddies like quills from trays of ink. A Canada jay chirps its little song, *tweet-tweet*, as a light breeze catches the river to make a silver patchwork of lace, a design for embroidery. And there are chunks of foam adrift: snowflakes, doilies, and fists of lamb's wool. My smoke drifts in a haze and makes a cocoon over the water. The air has prominent hollow sounds now before the rain. Out in the main stream, fish are jumping to nourish the interest of the men and make them shout at one another in accented monotones before settling down to fish again.

I huddle in reflection, going over some old poems I have read and now realize I must read again. The works trigger deeper and more meaningful images for me now: April as the cruellest month, the gathering of rosebuds, the tiring of the great harvest, and the queen of far-away all leave me contemplative on this wintry day. Familiar lines to re-read, reinterpret. You see, I have been a man of books, a man of images, an inside man. I have spent most of my life working on that part of myself. Now, at seventy-eight, I pride myself on the comfort I find in it. An old mind following old lines I once thought I understood, lines that have since taken on new meaning. I shield myself in this kind of meditation because it is so much warmer on the inside, for me.

Since you have gone (so long ago), and because you have gone, this is the only way I can find a small measure of comfort. To those on the outside I have become tiresome, a bore. I am poorly dressed and my ragged hair has threads of grey, which can be frightening, especially to the young who play out here on days like this. Today I am congested from the dampness. My knees and ankles ache from climbing slippery shores and wading among the bulrushes this fall. I cannot stand nor lay nor sit in comfort anymore. I long for genuine conversation, good food, beautiful music, and real friends.

The friends I search for inside myself because many have already gone, so that here on the darkening shores there is at least some light. For there is nowhere on earth as hollow and chilling as a river after all the leaves have come down and winter is approaching. Dark and blustery winter. The silent old river, a stream that flows from out of a rocky past toward an uncertain end.

Perhaps a small fire will take some of the storm fear out of this day, I think. A cup of tea. There are echoes in the hollow air as I gather spruce limbs and pine sticks that look like chicken bones to add to the blaze. To get my little fire going I have burned the index pages of Plato's *Republic* (but have savoured the sonnets of Shakespeare and Shelley, because I always see you somewhere in them).

With aching hands I have whittled a green sapling for a hanging stick and, for a teapot, I have fashioned a two-litre tin pail burnt black, with a handle of twisted wire. Having filled the pail with water from the brook, I hang it over the fire to boil. I sit on a rock and watch the water steam as the orange flames lick the base of the can to make it sing, then whistle and dance. As I feed more sticks under the pail, the flames snap and crack, sending smoke and cinders out over the river.

Finally, the water in the can begins to bubble in dancing bulbs of blown glass that splatter onto the flame, making it spit and sputter and puff. I fumble in the lunchbox for tea, Earl Grey, and toss three or four bags into the water to make an amber hiss and gurgle before using my claw-like hands to lift the tea and set it on a flat rock to steep and cool. (If it cools too quickly it will discolour the flavour.) It starts to rain softly, dimpling the tea and the river, which is smoother now that the wind has gone down.

I fumble through my pack for my old blue raincoat. Carefully, I wade out into the stream where they can hear me above the din of rapids, and I shout, "Tea time!" Then I struggle back to the fireside, my comfort zone. I build up the blaze, arrange tin mugs on a ledge, and set out brandy for sweetener and cream to soften the taste.

The fishers wander in, one at a time. They stand around and take off their gloves to hold their red and eager hands and rubber boots to the fire, until their felt soles begin to smell. They remark about the coolness here in Canada so early in the autumn. They talk of the fish they have seen in these pools on cool days like this and the fish they have risen on such-and-such a fly on this kind of day, in this kind of water. And they reminisce about previous trips—the ducks, deer, and bear they have killed in our country and in others on days just like this. And they speak of what a break they are having, away from their offices and away from their spouses, but they regret missing the ball scores and the results of trading on the stock exchange. They wonder if any new money has come in since they have left home. Still, they want to stretch the day into the night. For they are really nature lovers—woods people—they say.

McGill has a plan. He says he is going to poison all the coyotes in his province to help save the deer for the hunting season. *Dip wieners into gasoline and set them out on the low branches of trees.* Findlay is going to shoot all the ducks to help protect the fish. *Blast the hell out of every last one.* And Scaling is going to donate some money to the popular restoration groups, who will replenish the streams with tank fish so the fishing will be better down the road. Taylor says the whole problem is that there are too few trees in the woods. McGill thinks we have too many old-growth trees that consume the water, and this is why our rivers are getting smaller each year. They argue this point. Scaling thinks there should be more plantations, more uniform woods, perhaps all pine trees.

The men boast to each other about the great schools they attended and the alumni reunions coming up. They compare the great commencement speeches they have heard. Suddenly it is raining so hard that the stream is frosted over like crisper glass and I cannot see for the fog. As the rain comes straight down like weighted twines, it collects on the shoulders of my raincoat, which begins to leak. Water streams down my neck.

I pour the tea and offer a dash of brandy. They huddle to light their cigars from a twig held to the fire, then sip the steaming brew and talk in barks, laughing in sharp staccato bursts. They crowd each other to make room around the fire, room for themselves in the conversation, like children in front of an ice cream wagon. As the rain falls, it cools their tea and their cigars disintegrate and the ashes fall into the tin mugs. They move under a tree to keep the spirit alive, the spirit of this kind of day a day that I have long since tried to block out.

After being on the river so long, I have lost track of what day it really is. Is it Saturday or Sunday? At my age every day is Sunday, especially here on the river. Is this really the new age? And what stream is this? Is there still a stream, a country for me? Every day now seems to have a strange origin, and I struggle for the spirit of a familiar place. I was once an outdoor person myself. But I know this can never be again.

To go back is impossible, lest I go inside to where life is glorified by the changes that growth brings to a thing. Many my age are in this place that is forever beckoning to me now.

When the tea is almost gone, my guests slosh what is left onto the rocks, grab their tackle, and head back out into the river to jostle for position and start over. A Canada jay glides down on silent wing and tilts its little head in question, its eyes beads of glass. Having gained my trust, it hops up to me and I serve it crumbs like the Eucharist. Then I build up the fire, pour what tea is left into my cup, and turn my back to the river to look for shelter somewhere beneath the hemlock, to a place where I won't see this day for what it has become.

My internal images reappear in new dreams, and seasons long since gone come back to me. Nourished and guided in retrospect, they dance in a way that pleases me this time. Old enemies reconcile in a haze of memory, repaying me their debts with showers of accolades. They burn bright for a time, even glow, as if infused with a sudden impulse to care. And I embrace them, in a sense. The flames smoulder but twinkle in the rain as the smoke forms a cloud over the water and drifts upstream. I follow the images through the cruel rains of April and the lightning storms of summer to sometime after harvest, to this winter's day. Oh, it's just some kind of childish game I like to play. There is always new hope in a child, and that inner child in me is still full of energy and dreams.

I am very young, and once again the ice has begun to freeze along the shoreline bushes. "Board ice," my father calls it. A grey sky is closing down and snow is in the wind, already. Soon it will be scudding from out of the north to make patches of white on a slate scrolled by the blades of skates. Dawn forms in my eyes, a yellow and foggy fleece that is mesmerizing, and I am not sure which way to turn. I know it is Saturday morning and I am looking for the ice, my sister and I. Oxhana and Harold are coming down to join us. Everything is sparkling against the bright sunlight. Slipping and sliding, we are moving through the bent grass that crunches under our feet like frozen moss, leaving our tracks to dry and warm against the morning sun, making black footprints to be followed days and weeks later. The hawthorn berries have fallen, and the sun no longer warms us.

The first signs are the beads. We all notice the glass-like beads along the water's edge—frozen teardrops that have formed overnight in ragged grass. These beads glitter like a network of crystals with stems, brittle to the touch, between a river of iced tea and the straw-like shore grass that's still standing upright because we haven't had a real snow yet. We step on straw-lined test tubes and they snap. These test tubes and frozen teardrops melt and moisten the sand as the day warms, so that the shore is bare and dry again before dusk. Then the cycle repeats itself, slightly stronger each chilly morning we come to the river to look for ice, treading along with mindless banter.

Until one Saturday we find, in the unmoving shallows beneath the rushes, a plate of glass over the eddy. Strong and complete, frosted glass as thin as Cellophane in places, and thick as the smoky plastic used to cover our windows for winter in others. We jump on it to test its strength against rubber heels. We take off our mittens and pick up the angled pieces to look through them, first at the shadowy trees, then at the smaller, embroidered port plates that have formed overnight and move past to make a black-and-white conclave farther out. We stare at these and listen to them *shhhh*ing and bumping against one another, crowding into the channel in a reluctant yet hurried migration. Their edges have become furrowed and scalloped into fancy pie plates, until against the sun they grow apart as clear as moving pictures of the washed gravel beneath them. The pieces we are holding melt and drip on our sleeves, and we let them fall and break. A Saturday ritual.

There are snow flurries scattered in the wind when, on a morning in December, we test the board ice once again. First by throwing rocks, then by dropping a log. Would it be strong enough to skate on? Not near the outer edge, of course, but in the eddy itself we think it is. There have been no autumn rains so the water had not risen. And we know what is under the river ice here. We know the river will freeze across soon because it really is winter now. Any sooner would have been bad luck, for if it freezes across in November, according to our parents, it is certain to go out again and make "a helluva mess."

We watch the board ice thicken, watch the powdery bottom grow lifeless beneath it and the tiny fish disappear and the waving eelgrass fade to black strings of twine. The plates that move past grow bigger and bigger and move more slowly, until the whole concern is a world of moving craters. We know it will stop one night and freeze solid. Then, after a day or two, someone will pick their way across for the first time, and with the axe put the tiny bushes in a staggered row for us to follow.

Finally, seeing that the board ice is strong in close, we run home for our skates and return to the shore, out of breath. We sit on mittens placed on flat boulders along the shore to tie our skates. Then stand on unsure ankles, our unsure young selves. Using a twisted tree branch for support, we move about in small circles. We begin in straight lines, then zigzag to chase one another. We bump and fall down and get up to try again. We scream and laugh so our fathers and mothers can hear us from home. We gather alder skeletons from the hillside and build our Saturday bonfire. With the heel of a discarded rubber boot and some tree branches, we play *Hockey Night in Canada* right out there on the board ice. Just a foolish outdoor game, that's all it is.

My father comes down to tell us supper is ready. He says the upper eddy is better; it has fewer rocks when the water is this low. I tell him about the twenty-five goals I scored.

My sister and I follow him home, across fields of frozen cow tracks now sprinkled with salt. We mope along on tired ankles where the winding trails of mud are black cement, then through our garden, honeycombed now. I see Oxhana climbing the hill to the Hlodan farm across the river. I see Harold undressing in the slanting, cluttered home that he and his mother share. In our own summer kitchen, a Christmas tree stands in a pail. Father has cut and dragged it from the swamp this very day. The old board floor of the shed cracks and snaps under our feet as we go inside to a supper we have been smelling for hours from the river.

And then, as if to take the place of board ice and hockey, or even a family meal, you appear front and centre, my sweet and tender Oxhana, just as you always do. You are still mysterious but commanding, even at this rugged age, "that time of year thou mayst in me behold." And I see you sitting there by the fire, the way you used to do in that old farmhouse, with curtains drawn against the night. Your knees are pulled up under your skirt to make a tent that covers your ankles. Your thin bare feet are resting on the edge of an empty chair, hair long over your shoulders. And your dark eyes are moving me. Even now. I share your lighted candle, hear your chamber music as you get up, and once again we move together in a kind of dance.

Rain turns to hail and filters among the trees to hop about on dead leaves and hiss in the moving river and make my bonfire smoulder. Once again you have helped me block out the hollowness, the rain, the approaching darkness. I wait for the night with an indifference that only borders on sanity. While in the trees, the little jay chirps *tweet-tweet*, its ruffled plumage delicate now upon bare limbs. It teeters in the storm, its tail feathers the mark of a broom in swept snow.

CHRISTMAS IN A SNOWDRIFT

Greta Gaskin Bidlake

"Tell you about how I once spent part of Christmas Day in a snowdrift?" queried Uncle Robert Clark, settling into his easy chair before the fire and preparing to tell the children's favourite story.

Well, when I was a boy we lived in a hilly country around Cedar Creek. Dreadful storms we used to have when the snow would drift into the ravines and gullies 'til the roads would be blocked for days. It was cold too; the wind came whistling between the hills and swept down the valleys, making a blizzard out of everything but the mildest storms.

Father had a hired man who had been with us for years. He was treated like one of the family and everybody called him Dan. Now, Dan was handy with a hammer and saw, and when Father took the contract for driving the weekly mail between our settlement and Hillside it fell mostly to Dan's lot to do the actual driving so he built an old-fashioned contrivance, a big covered box that fastened on a low sled. The children along the road used to laugh when he went by and called it "Dan's goose house" but to me it could not have been more wonderful if it had been a prairie schooner on runners. I was proud as could be whenever Dan overtook me on the way home from school and gave me a ride.

You can imagine, then, how I felt when Father told me Dan was going into the city the day before Christmas and said I could go too.

It was my birthday and this was to be my special birthday treat. Winter had set in early that fall and scarcely a week passed that the men did not have to turn out with teams, shovels, sleds, and break out the road. I went outdoors a dozen times after Father told me and scanned the sky to see if it was going to storm. It didn't look any too promising, but when they roused me out before daylight the next morning I tumbled down into the kitchen where a breakfast of pork and pancakes was cooking. Father said the wind was right for a storm, but it had moderated some, so he guessed it wouldn't amount to much; we needed groceries and Dan would have to go anyway.

It was just coming daylight when we started. The city was eighteen miles away and we didn't go very often. The sled looked prepared for a real important journey too, let me tell you. There was a little door in the side and a big pane of glass in front that slid up and down. Dan could leave this open or close it up and still keep the reins in his hand as they ran through a slit cut below the sash. The bottom of the sled was piled with hay, there was half a sack of oats for the horse; we had two fur robes, a charcoal burner to keep us warm when the sled front was open, and I had a big slab of hot soapstone that Mother had heated for my feet. Besides this we had lunch and a can of hot tea. Old Gray was harnessed with strong traces and a stout collar and hames for pulling us through the drifts, and Dan put a shovel and axe into the sled the last thing before leaving.

The roads were fairly good with only a bit of heavy going here and there, for they had been well travelled since the last storm. Old Gray carefully wallowed through these. We had brought him in preference to any of the other horses because he was a calm old plodder who never got excited in heavy drifts and pulled without breaking the harness or upsetting the sled. It was a clear morning and the old horse jogged along over the good stretches, shaking the shaft bells into a jolly, jingling tune. My spirits rose high with the fun and adventure of the trip. I had never been to town in winter before.

But it was slow going on the whole, and when we still had some miles before us the sky became overcast and the wind rose a little with a chill nip that made Dan look anxious. I could see the town lying—blanketed with snow, spires rising, chimneys smoking—on the other side of the river in the distance. It lay all crystal and white like an enchanted city of a kingdom in Arabian nights.

The first flakes of the storm were falling as we drove along its streets. Dan went at once to the marketplace where he gave Old Gray a drink at the street fountain, then stabled him in an old barn in the backyard of one of the houses nearby. When he came back to the sled we sat inside, the coziest of campers, to eat our bread and cold meat and drink our tea. I was hungry after our early breakfast and long ride and my, how good it tasted!

We then set out to visit the stores. I'll never forget how wonderful everything seemed to me! The hard-packed streets, the crowds streaming to and fro, the small boys running about among them, the long counters in the stores piled high with Christmas wares with fascinating selections from the choicest stock displayed in the windows, and the soft thick flakes falling over it all. To a country boy like me, it was fairyland come true. I bought a pair of scissors for Mother, a large cake of scented shaving soap for father, and a big bright handkerchief for Dan. I sunk the rest of my money into a huge bag of nuts and candy.

Dan had ordered the groceries meanwhile and now we had but one more errand to do. Father had charged Dan to take a letter to Judge White and bring back an answer. That took us over to the other end of the city. We went on a horse-car and I couldn't help thinking how much it was like our sled. When we reached the judge's house he was not at home and we had to wait an hour or so 'til he came. He read our letter, went into the library to answer it, and did not reappear for half an hour. As soon as he came out again Dan rose, cap in hand, ready to go. The large flakes fell soft and thick as we walked down the steps.

Dan collected our parcels, put them in the sled, and gave Old Gray another feed of oats. Then he went into the house for the soapstone, which the woman had kindly offered to heat up again in her oven, and she made us both come in for a cup of tea and some doughnuts.

It was well on toward the middle of the afternoon when we got started back and the going was getting worse all the time. Dan kept Old Gray jogging along smartly and I saw him frown anxiously at the weather once or twice. I was so blissfully happy and the sled was such a comfortable place that I soon nestled down among the fur robes and fell asleep to the tune of the jingling bells and a song about a bear fight Dan used to sing.

Sometimes I half awoke, usually when the sled slowed up, and peeking out from under the bearskin I could tell by the half light coming in through the window that we were passing along the bottom of a deep and narrow trench cut through one of the high drifts. The walls, I knew, rose high above us on both sides. Now and then we met another team and I listened sleepily while Dan and the passing driver exchanged remarks. Twice Old Gray stopped and Dan had to get out and shovel a way through the drifts. It came twilight when we were still five miles from home; darkness fell almost immediately after and I was awakened by the sudden stopping of the sled and Dan talking to Old Gray.

I sat up. Dan had climbed out the little door and gone ahead with the shovel. High snow walls rose on each side, so near I could touch them by sticking out my hand. Old Gray had tugged us through this far but now he stood stock-still, refusing to budge. Soon Dan came back to the sled.

"We've passed the branch road and there's nothin' but drifts from now on," said he. "Can't shovel through the whole of them and besides, 'tain't likely we can keep to the road along the stretch of marsh ahead. Looks like we have ter stay right where we be."

"Stay here all night, Dan!" I cried.

As I remember it I wasn't scared a mite. I just thought what fun it would be. Of course if Dan said we were going to do it, it must be that we could. I had all a child's faith—I knew he would keep me safe.

"I reckon that's about what it amounts to," answered Dan. "Don't be frightened, Robbie. I'll fix you up fine. We can't get no further 'til morning and anyways this is the best place to stop."

"Huh! I'm not frightened," I sniffed scornfully. "And, say, Dan, isn't this an adventure—a little one, I mean?"

"Well, yes, I'll allow it is," said Dan. "It's a pretty big adventure for a small boy. Now, Robbie, we have got to be quick; it's as dark as pitch and time we was fixed up for the night. Hand me that axe."

I watched out the window and saw what Dan did. He first unhitched Old Gray. Then he tied the shafts of the sled so they stuck straight up and turned Old Gray to face the window in the front of the sled. Then he climbed up the snowbank, axe and lantern in hand, and disappeared, coming back in a few minutes with an armful of branches from a patch of woods nearby. Two or three times he did this. The last trip he brought in poles which he stuck in the snow at the corners of a square. He stuck the biggest branches upright between them all the way around, made a floor, and built a roof, both of fir branches. Old Gray now had a shelter of his own, three sides were fir branches and the fourth formed by our sled. Dan gave him an armful of hay out of the sled and tied our deerskin rug over him. Old Gray seemed as snug and contented as at home in his warm stable. Dan came in where I was then. We lit the charcoal burner, ate the rest of our lunch, heated up the tea in our tin cups, and curled up together under the big bearskin robe.

I lay awake for a little while thinking what a strange Christmas Eve this was. I wouldn't have missed it for worlds, but I wondered what was going on at home and would they hang up my stocking for me?

Every Christmas Eve I could remember I had hung up a stocking on the mantel of the sitting-room fireplace. We got old-fashioned gifts in those days: animals fried of doughnut dough and sugared; warmly knit mittens, stockings, and scarves; cakes of maple sugar molded into churches, houses, and other queer shapes; a bit of brown sugar candy thickly sprinkled with butternuts; a toy or two whittled by someone clever with a jackknife. That was all—except, perhaps, for some peppermints or some other little unexpected store treat—but we were just as happy as children nowadays, and I sometimes think Christmas meant more to us than it does to youngsters today.

I soon dozed off, however, lulled by the wind and Dan's even snoring. He was tired after wading around through the drifts and fairly shook the sides of the "goose house" with his great, deep, regular breaths.

When I awoke it was morning and the stars were out. Old Gray's head was nosing at the steamy, frosted window and he began to whinny when he heard us moving about. Dan broke into a big bag of soda crackers Mother had sent for and we had some for our breakfast. After that he went out with the shovel to scout around.

"I reckon we'll get home to that big fat Christmas goose sometime today, sonny," he comforted cheerily on his return, "and a cracker breakfast will just sharpen our appetites. Now, the next thing is—just how we goin' to git there? It's too deep to go across the fields," he continued. "I thought mebee we could follow Jud Foster's fence from here and take a shortcut in. If I had a light pung I'd try it, but with this heavy sled it don't seem likely. I'm goin' to start shovellin' and I calculate someone'll be along to meet us sometime today if it is Christmas. They got to keep the road clear for the doctor to get into Old Man Trimble, recollect."

When I saw he had the way clear the whole length of the tunnel I ran out to stretch my legs. Shouts sounded beyond, coming to us across the marsh and the crack of ox-whips on the frozen air. There they were—half a dozen teams, their drivers dressed in fur caps and armed with shovels! I shouted and waved my long red scarf. Dan had gone back to get Old Gray hitched up and I ran to help. We had him in the shafts again in less than ten minutes and we met the breaking-out party on the marsh.

Father turned about and I rode back with him on the ox sled. Every now and then Father would stop me for a minute while he called ahead some question to Dan and Dan shouted back. I knew the best of the adventure was over—except, of course, for my relating it in triumph to envious schoolmates who had never enjoyed a night camping in Dan's "goose house"—but I was still happy, and not a little hungry.

How good it was to get back into our warm, cheerful kitchen and smell the goose roasting in the oven, the mince pie steaming in a boiler on the stove! The air was full of scents: spices and savoury. Mother was setting the table when I went in and we agreed to let my bulging stockings wait till after dinner. I was kissed, and teased, and joked, of course, about how near I had come to spending the whole of Christmas Day in a snowdrift, but I laughed back, handed around my Christmas presents, and capped the situation by a request long simmering in my brain.

"Say, Father, when my next birthday comes, may I go again?"

WINTER DOG
Alistair MacLeod

I am writing this in December. In the period close to Christmas, and three days after the first snowfall in this region of southwestern Ontario. The snow came quietly in the night or in the early morning. When we went to bed near midnight, there was none at all. Then early in the morning we heard the children singing Christmas songs from their rooms across the hall. It was very dark and I rolled over to check the time. It was 4:30 A.M. One of them must have awakened and looked out the window to find the snow and then eagerly awakened the other. They are half crazed by the promise of Christmas, and the discovery of the snow is an unexpected giddy surprise. There was no snow promised for this area, not even yesterday.

"What are you doing?" I call, although it is obvious.

"Singing Christmas songs," they shout back with equal obviousness, "because it snowed."

"Try to be quiet," I say, "or you'll wake the baby."

"She's already awake," they say. "She's listening to our singing. She likes it. Can we go out and make a snowman?"

I roll from my bed and go to the window. The neighbouring houses are muffled in snow and silence and there are as yet no lights in any of them. The snow has stopped falling and its whitened quietness reflects the shadows of the night.

"This snow is no good for snowmen," I say. "It is too dry."

"How can snow be dry?" asks a young voice.

Then an older one says, "Well, then can we go out and make the first tracks?"

They take my silence for consent and there are great sounds rustling and giggling as they go downstairs to touch the light switches and rummage and jostle for coats and boots.

"What on earth is happening?" asks my wife from her bed. "What are they doing?"

"They are going outside to make the first tracks in the snow," I say. "It snowed quite heavily last night."

"What time is it?"

"Shortly after four-thirty."

"Oh."

We ourselves have been nervous and restless for the past weeks. We have been troubled by illness and uncertainty in those we love far away on Canada's east coast. We have already considered and rejected driving the fifteen hundred miles. Too far, too uncertain, too expensive, fickle weather, the complications of transporting Santa Claus.

Instead, we sleep uncertainly and toss in unbidden dreams. We jump when the phone rings after 10:00 P.M. and are then reassured by the distant voices.

"First of all, there is nothing wrong," they say. "Things are just the same."

Sometimes we make calls ourselves, even to the hospital in Halifax, and are surprised at the voices which answer.

"I just got here this afternoon from Newfoundland. I'm going to try to stay a week. He seems better today. He's sleeping now."

At other times we receive calls from farther west, from Edmonton and Calgary and Vancouver. People hoping to find objectivity in the most subjective of situations. Strung out in uncertainty across the time zones from British Columbia to Newfoundland.

Within our present city, people move and consider possibilities:

If he dies tonight we'll leave right away. Can you come?
We will have to drive as we'll never get air reservations at this time.

*I'm not sure my car is good enough. I'm always afraid of
the mountains near Cabano.
If we were stranded in Rivière du Loup we would be
worse off than being here. It would be too far for anyone
to come and get us.
My car will go but I'm not so sure I can drive it all the
way. My eyes are not so good anymore, especially at night
in drifting snow.
Perhaps there'll be no drifting snow.
There's always drifting snow.
We'll take my car if you'll drive it. We'll have to drive
straight through.
John phoned and said he'll give us his car if we want it or
he'll drive—either his own car or someone else's.
He drinks too heavily, especially for long-distance
driving, and at this time of year. He's been drinking ever
since this news began.
He drinks because he cares. It's just the way he is. Not
everybody drinks.
Not everybody cares, and if he gives you his word, he'll
never drink until he gets there. We all know that.*

But so far nothing has happened. Things seem to remain the same.

Through the window and out on the white plane of the snow, the silent, laughing children now appear. They move in their muffled clothes like mummers on the whitest of stages. They dance and gesture noiselessly, flopping their arms in parodies of heavy, happy, earthbound birds. They have been warned by the eldest to be aware of the sleeping neighbours so they cavort only in pantomime, sometimes raising mittened hands to their mouths to suppress their joyous laughter. They dance and prance in the moonlight, tossing snow in one another's direction, tracing out various shapes and initials, forming lines that snake across the previously unmarked whiteness. All of it in silence, unknown and unseen and unheard to the neighbouring world. They seem unreal even to me, their father, standing at his darkened window. It is almost as if they have danced out of the world of folklore like happy elves who cavort and mimic and caper through the private hours of this whitened dark, only to vanish with the coming of the morning's light and leaving only the signs of their activities behind. I am tempted to check the recently vacated beds to confirm what perhaps I think I know.

Then out of the corner of my eye I see him. The golden collie-like dog. He appears almost as if from the wings of the stage, or as a figure newly noticed in the lower corner of a winter painting. He sits quietly and watches the playful scene before him and then, as if responding to a silent invitation, bounds into its midst. The children chase him in frantic circles, falling and rolling as he doubles back and darts and dodges between their legs and through their outstretched arms. He seizes a mitt loosened from its owner's hand, and tosses it happily in the air and then snatches it back into his jaws an instant before it reaches the ground and seconds before the tumbling bodies fall on the emptiness of its expected destination. He races to the edge of the scene and lies facing them, holding the mitt tantalizingly between his paws, and then as they dash towards him, he leaps forward again, tossing and catching it before him and zigzagging through them as the Sunday football player might return the much sought-after ball. After he has gone through and eluded them all, he looks back over his shoulder and again, like an elated athlete, tosses the mitt high in what seems like an imaginary end zone. Then he seizes it once more and lopes in a wide circle around his pursuers, eventually coming closer and closer to them until once more their stretching hands are able to actually touch his shoulders and back and haunches, although he continues always to wiggle free. He is touched but never captured, which is the nature of the game. Then he is gone. As suddenly as he came. I strain my eyes in the direction of the adjoining street, towards the house where I have often seen him, always within a yard enclosed by woven links of chain. I see the flash of his silhouette, outlined perhaps against the snow or the light cast by the street lamps or the moon. It arcs upwards and seems to hang for an instant high above the top of the fence and then it descends on the other side. He lands on his shoulder in a fluff of snow and with a half roll regains his feet and vanishes within the shadow of his owner's house.

"What are you looking at?" asks my wife.

"That golden collie-like dog from the other street was just playing with the children in the snow."

"But he's always in that fenced-in yard."

"I guess not always. He jumped the fence just now and went back in. I guess the owners and the rest of us think he's fenced in but he knows he's not. He probably comes out every night and leads an exciting life. I hope they don't see his tracks they'll probably begin to chain him."

"What are the children doing?"

"They look tired now from chasing the dog. They'll probably soon be back in. I think I'll go downstairs and wait for them and make myself a cup of coffee."

"Okay."

I look once more towards the fenced-in yard but the dog is nowhere to be seen.

I first saw such a dog when I was twelve and he came as pup of about two months in a crate to the railroad station which was about eight miles from where we lived. Someone must have phoned or dropped in to say, "Your dog's at the station."

He had come to Cape Breton in response to a letter and a cheque which my father had sent to Morrisburg, Ontario. We had seen the ads for "cattle collie dogs" in the *Family Herald*, which was the farm newspaper of the time, and we were need of a good young working dog.

His crate was clean and neat and there was still a supply of dog biscuits with him and a can in the corner to hold water. The baggage handlers had looked after him well on the trip east, and he appeared in good spirits. He had a white collar and chest and four rather large white paws and a small white blaze on his forehead. The rest of him was a fluffy, golden brown, although his eyebrows and the tips of his ears as well as the end of his tail were darker, tingeing almost to black. When he grew to his full size the blackish shadings became really black, and although he had the long, heavy coat of a collie, it was in certain areas more grey than gold. He was also taller than the average collie and with a deeper chest. He seemed to be at least part German shepherd.

It was winter when he came and we kept him in the house where he slept behind the stove in a box lined with an old coat. Our other dogs slept mostly in the stables or outside in the woodpiles or under porches or curled up on the banking of the house. We seemed to care more for him because he was smaller and it was winter and he was somehow like a visitor, and also because more was expected of him and also perhaps cause we had paid money for him and thought about his coming for some time—like a "planned" child. Skeptical neighbours and relatives who thought the idea of paying money for a dog was rather exotic or frivolous would ask, "Is that your Ontario dog" or "Do you think your Ontario dog will be any good?"

He turned out to be no good at all and no one knew why. Perhaps it was because of the suspected German shepherd blood. But he could not "get the hang of it." Although we worked him and trained him as we had other dogs, he seemed always to bring panic instead of order and to make things worse instead of better. He became a "head dog," which meant in instead of working behind the cattle, he lunged at their heads, impeding them from any forward motion and causing them to turn in endless, meaningless bewildered circles.

On the few occasions when he did go behind them, he was "rough," which meant that instead of being a floating, nipping, suggestive presence, he actually bit them and caused them to gallop, which was another sin. Sometimes in the summer the milk cows suffering from his misunderstood pursuit would jam pell-mell into the stable, tossing their wide horns in fear, and with their great sides heaving and perspiring while down their legs and tails the wasted milk ran in rivulets mingling with the blood caused by his slashing wounds. He was, it was said, "worse than nothing."

Gradually everyone despaired, although he continued to grow grey and golden and was, as everyone agreed, a beautiful-looking dog.

He was also tremendously strong. In the winter months I would hitch him to a sleigh, which he pulled easily and willingly on almost any surface. When he was harnessed I used to put a collar around his neck and attach a light line to it so I might have some minimum control over him, but it was hardly ever needed. He would pull home the Christmas tree or the bag of flour or the deer that was shot far back in the woods; and when we visited our winter snares he would pull home the gunnysacks containing the partridges and rabbits.

He would also pull us, especially on the flat windswept stretches of land beside the sea. There the snow was never really deep and the water that oozed from a series of freshwater springs and ponds contributed to a glaze of ice and crisply crusted snow, which the sleigh runners seemed to sing over without ever breaking through. He would begin with an easy lope and then increase his swiftness until both he and the sleigh seemed to touch the surface at only irregular intervals. He would stretch out then with his ears flattened against his head and his shoulders bunching and contracting in the rhythm of his speed. Behind him on the sleigh we would cling tenaciously to the wooden slats as the particles of ice and snow dislodged by his nails hurtled towards our faces. We would avert our heads and close our eyes and the wind stung so sharply that the difference between freezing and burning could not be known. He would do that until late in the afternoon when it was time to return home and begin our chores.

On the sunny winter Sunday I am thinking of, I planned to visit my snares. There seemed no other children around that afternoon and the adults were expecting relatives. I harnessed the dog to the sleigh, opened the door of the house, and shouted that I was going to look at my snares. We began to climb the hill behind the house on our way to the woods when we looked back and out towards the sea.

The "big ice," which was what we called the major pack of drift ice, was in solidly against the shore and stretched out beyond the range of vision. It had not been in yesterday, although for the past weeks we had seen it moving offshore, sometimes close and sometimes distant, depending on the winds and tides. The coming of the big ice marked the official beginning of the coldest part of winter. It was mostly drift ice from the Arctic and Labrador, although some of it was freshwater ice from the estuary of the St. Lawrence. It drifted down with the dropping temperatures, bringing its own mysterious coldness and stretching for hundreds of miles in craters and pans, sometimes in grotesque shapes and sometimes in dazzling architectural forms. It was blue and white and sometimes grey, and at other times a dazzling emerald green.

The dog and I changed our direction toward the sea, to find what the ice might yield. Our land had always been beside the sea and we had always gone toward it to find newness and the extraordinary. Over the years we, as others along the coast, had found quite a lot, although never the pirate chests of gold that were supposed to abound, or the reasons for the mysterious lights that our elders still spoke of and persisted in seeing. But kegs of rum had washed up, and sometime bloated horses and various fishing paraphernalia and valuable timber and furniture from foundered ships. The door of my room was apparently the galley door from a ship called the *Judith Franklin*, which was wrecked during the early winter in which my great-grandfather was building his house. My grandfather told of how they had heard the cries and seen the lights as the ship neared the rocks and of how they had run down in the dark and tossed line to the people while tying themselves to trees on the shore. All were saved, including women clinging to small children. The next day the builders of the new house went down to the shore and salvaged what they could from the wreckage of the vanquished ship. A sort of symbolic marriage of the new and the old: doors and shelving, stairways, hatches, wooden chests, and trunks and various glass figurines and lanterns, which were miraculously never broken.

People came too. The dead as well as the living. Bodies of men swept overboard and reported lost at sea and the bodies of men still crouched within the shelter of their boats' broken bows. And sometimes in late winter young sealers who had quit their vessels would walk across the ice and come to our doors. They were usually very young—some still in their teens—and had signed on for jobs they could not or no longer wished to handle. They were often disoriented and did not know where they were, only that they had seen land and had decided to walk towards it. They were often frostbitten and with little money and uncertain as to how they might get to Halifax. The dog and I walked towards the ice upon the sea.

Sometimes it was hard to "get on" the ice, which meant that at the point where the pack met the shore there might be open water or irregularities caused by the indentations of the coastline or the workings of the tides and currents, but for us on that day there was no difficulty at all. We were "on" easily and effortlessly and enthused in our new adventure. For the first mile there was nothing but the vastness of the white expanse. We came to a clear stretch where the ice was as smooth and unruffled as that of an indoor arena, and I knelt on the sleigh while the dog loped easily along. Gradually the ice changed to an uneven terrain of pressure ridges and hummocks, making it impossible to ride farther; and then suddenly, upon rounding a hummock, I saw the perfect seal.

At first I thought it was alive, as did the dog, who stopped so suddenly in his tracks that the sleigh almost collided with his legs. The hackles on the back of his neck rose and he growled in the dangerous way he was beginning to develop. But the seal was dead, yet facing us in a frozen perfection that was difficult to believe. There was a light powder of snow over its darker coat and a delicate rime of frost still formed the outline of its whiskers. Its eyes were wide open and it stared straight ahead toward the land. Even now in memory it seems more real than reality—as if it were transformed by frozen art into something more arresting than life itself. The way the sudden seal in the museum exhibit freezes your eyes with the touch of truth. Immediately I wanted to take it home.

It was frozen solidly in a base of ice so I began to look for thing that might serve as a pry. I let the dog out of his harness and hung the sleigh and harness on top of the hummock to mark the place and began my search. Some distance away I found a pole about twelve feet long. It is always surprising to find such things on the ice field but they are—often amazingly—there, almost in the same way that you might find a pole floating in the summer ocean. Unpredictable but possible. I took the pole back and began my work. The dog went off on explorations of his own.

Although it was firmly frozen, the task did not seem impossible. By inserting the end of the pole under first one side and the other and working from front to back, it was possible to cause a gradual loosening. I remember thinking how very warm it was because I was working hard and perspiring—heavily. When the dog came back he was uneasy, and I realized it was starting to snow a bit but I was almost done. He sniffed with disinterest at the seal and began to whine a bit, something he did not often do.

Finally, after another quarter of an hour, I was able to roll my trophy onto the sleigh and with the dog in his harness we set off. We had gone perhaps two hundred yards when the seal slid free. I took the dog and the sleigh back and once again managed to roll the seal on. This time I took the line from the dog's collar and tied the seal to the sleigh, reasoning that the dog would go home anyway and there would be no need to guide him. My fingers were numb as I tried to fasten the awkward knots and the dog began to whine and rear. When I gave the command he bolted forward and I clung at the back of the sleigh to the seal. The snow was heavier now and blowing in my face but we were moving rapidly and when we came to the stretch of arena-like ice, we skimmed across it almost like an iceboat, the profile of the frozen seal at the front of the sleigh like those figures at the prows of Viking ships.

At the very end of the smooth stretch, we went through.

From my position at the end of the sleigh I felt him drop almost before I saw him, and rolled backwards seconds before the sleigh and seal followed him into the blackness of the water. He went under once carried by his own momentum but surfaced almost immediately with his head up and his paws scrambling at the icy, jagged edge of the hole; but when the weight and momentum of the sleigh and its burden struck, he went down again, this time out of sight.

I realized we had struck a "seam" and the stretch of smooth ice that had been deceivingly and temporarily joined to the rougher ice near the shore was now in the process of breaking away. I saw the widening line before me and jumped to the other side just as his head miraculously came up once more. I lay on my stomach and grabbed his collar in both my hands and then in a moment of panic did not know what to do. I could feel myself sliding towards him and the darkness of the water and was aware of the weight that pulled me forward and down. I was also aware of his razor-sharp claws flailing violently before my face and knew that I might lose my eyes. And I was aware that his own eyes were bulging from their sockets and that he might think I was trying to choke him and might lunge and slash my face with his teeth in desperation. I knew all of this but somehow did nothing about it; it seemed almost simpler to hang on and be drawn into the darkness of the gently slopping water, seeming to slop gently in spite of all the agitation. Then suddenly he was free, scrambling over my shoulder and dragging the sleigh behind him.

The seal surfaced again, buoyed up perhaps by the physics of its frozen body or the nature of its fur. Still looking more genuine than it could have in life, its snout and head broke the open water and it seemed to look at us curiously for an instant before it vanished permanently beneath the ice. The loose and badly tied knots had apparently not held when the sleigh was in a near-vertical position and we were saved by the ineptitude of my own numbed fingers. We had been spared for a future time.

He lay gasping and choking for a moment, coughing up the icy salt water, and then almost immediately his coat began to freeze. I realized then how cold I was myself and that even in the moments I had been lying on the ice, my clothes had begun to adhere to it. My earlier heated perspiration was now a cold rime upon my body and I imagined it outlining me there, beneath my clothes, in a sketch of frosty white. I got on the sleigh once more and crouched low as he began to race towards home. His coat was freezing fast, and as he ran the individual ice-coated hairs began to clack together like rhythmical castanets attuned to the motion of his body. It was snowing quite heavily in our faces now and it seemed to be approaching dusk, although I doubted if it were so on the land, which I could now no longer see.

I realized all the obvious things I should have considered earlier. That if the snow was blowing in our faces, the wind was off the land, and if it was off the land, it was blowing the ice pack back out to sea. That was probably one reason the seam had opened. And also the ice had only been "in" one night and had not had a chance to set. I realized other things as well. That it was the time of the late afternoon when the tide was falling. That no one knew where we were. That I had said we were going to look at snares, which was not where we had gone at all. And I remembered now that I had received no answer even to that misinformation, so perhaps I had not even been heard. And also if there was drifting snow like this on land, our tracks would by now have been obliterated.

We came to a rough section of ice: huge slabs on their sides and others piled one on top of the other as if they were in some strange form of storage. It was no longer possible to ride the sleigh but as I stood up I lifted it and hung on to it as a means of holding on to the dog. The line usually attached to his collar had sunk with the vanished seal. My knees were stiff when I stood up. Deprived of the windbreak effect that the dog had provided, I felt the snow driving full into my face, particularly my eyes. It did not merely impede my vision the way distant snow flurries might, but actually entered my eyes, causing them to water and freeze nearly shut. I was aware of the weight of ice on my eyelashes and could see them as they gradually lowered and became heavier. I did not remember ice like this when I got on, although I did not find that terribly surprising. I pressed the soles of my numb feet firmly down upon it to try and feel if it was moving out, but it was impossible to tell because there was no fixed point of reference. Almost the sensation one gets on a conveyor belt at airports or on escalators; although you are standing still you recognize motion, but should you shut your eyes and be deprived of sight, even that recognition may become ambiguously uncertain.

The dog began to whine and to walk around me in circles, binding my legs with the traces of the harness as I continued to grasp the sleigh. Finally I decided to let him go as there seemed no way to hold him and there was nothing else to do. I unhitched the traces and doubled them up as best I could and tucked them under the back pad of his harness so they would drag behind him and become snagged on any obstacles. I did not take off my mitts to do so as I was afraid I would not be able to get them back on. He vanished into the snow almost immediately.

The sleigh had been a gift from an uncle, so I hung on to it and carried it with both hands before me like an ineffectual shield against the wind and snow. I lowered my head as much as I could and turned it sideways so the wind would beat against my head instead of directly into my face. Sometimes I turned and walked backwards for a few steps. Although I knew it was not the wisest thing to do, it seemed at times the way to breathe.

And then I began to feel the water sloshing about my feet.

Sometimes when the tides or currents ran heavily and the ice began to separate, the water that was beneath it would well up and wash over it, almost as if it were re-flooding. Sometimes you could see the hard ice clearly beneath the water, but at other times a sort of floating slush was formed mingling with snow and "slob" ice, which was not yet solid. It was thick and dense and soupy and it was impossible to see what lay beneath it. Experienced men on the ice sometimes carried a slender pole so they could test the consistency of the footing, but I was obviously not one of them—although I had a momentary twinge for the pole I had used to dislodge the seal. Still, there was nothing to do but go forward.

When I went through, the first sensation was almost of relief and relaxation for the water initially made me feel much warmer than I had been on the surface. It was the most dangerous of false sensations for I knew my clothes were becoming heavier by the second. I clung to the sleigh somewhat as a raft and lunged forward with it in a kind of up-and-down swimming motion, hoping that it might strike some sort of solidity before my arms became so weighted and sodden I could no longer lift them. I cried out then for the first time into the driving snow.

He came almost immediately, although I could see he was afraid and the slobbing slush was up to his knees. Still, he seemed to be on some kind of solid footing for he was not swimming. I splashed towards him and when almost there, desperately threw the sleigh before me and lunged for the edge of what seemed like his footing, but it only gave way as if my hands were closing on icy insubstantial porridge.

He moved forward then, although I still could not tell if what supported him would be of any use to me. Finally I grasped the breast strap of his harness. He began to back up then, and as I said, he was tremendously strong. The harness began to slide forward on his shoulders but he continued to pull as I continued to grasp and then I could feel my elbows on what seemed solid ice and I was able to hook them on the edge and draw myself, dripping and soaking, like another seal out of black water and onto the whiteness of the slushy ice. Almost at once my clothes began to freeze. My elbows and knees creaked when I bent them as if I were a robot from the realm of science fiction and then I could see myself clothed in transparent ice as if I had been coated with shellac or finished with a clear varnish.

As the fall into the winter sea had at first seemed ironically warm, so now my garments of ice seemed a protection against the biting wind. But I knew it was a deceptive sensation and I did not have much time before me. The dog faced the wind and I followed him. This time he stayed in sight, and at times even turned back to wait for me. He was cautious but certain and gradually the slush disappeared, and although we were still in water, the ice was hard and clear beneath it. The frozen heaviness of my clothes began to weigh on me and I could feel myself, ironically, perspiring within my suit of armour. I was very tired, which I knew was another dangerous sensation.

And then I saw the land.

It was very close and a sudden surprise. Almost like coming upon a stalled and unexpected automobile in a highway's winter storm. It was only yards away, and although there was no longer any ice actually touching the shore, there were several pans of it floating in the region between. The dog jumped from one to the other and I followed him, still clutching the sleigh, missing only the last pan floating close to the rocky shore. The water came only to my waist and I was able to touch the bottom and splash noisily to land. We had been spared again for a future time and I was never to know whether he had reached the shore himself and come back or whether he had heard my call against the wind.

We began to run towards home and the land lightened and there were touches of evening sun. The wind still blew but no snow was falling. Yet when I looked back, the ice and the ocean were invisible in the swirling squalls. It was like looking at another far and distant country on the screen of a snowy television.

I became obsessed—now that I could afford the luxury—with being found disobedient or considered a fool. The visitors' vehicles were still in the yard so I imagined most of the family to be in the parlour or living room, and I circled the house and entered through the kitchen, taking the dog with me. I was able to get upstairs unnoticed and get my clothes changed and when I came down I mingled with everybody and tried to appear as normal as I could. My own family was caught up with the visitors and only general comments came my way. The dog, who could not change his clothes, lay under the table with his head on his paws and he was also largely unnoticed. Later, as the ice melted from his coat, a puddle formed around him, which I casually mopped up. Still later someone said, "I wonder where that dog has been, his coat is soaking wet." I was never to tell anyone of the afternoon's experience or that he had saved my life.

Two winters later I was sitting at a neighbour's kitchen table when I looked out the window and saw the dog as he was shot.

He had followed my father and also me and had been sitting rather regally on a little hill beside the house and I suppose had presented an ideal target. But he had moved at just the right or wrong time and instead of killing him the high-powered bullet smashed into his shoulder. He jumped into the air and turned his snapping teeth upon the wound, trying to bite the cause of the pain he could not see. And then he turned towards home, unsteady but still strong on three remaining legs. No doubt he felt, as we all do, that if he could get home he might be saved. But he did not make it, as we knew he could not, because of the amount of blood on the snow and the wavering pattern of his three-legged tracks. Yet he was, as I said, tremendously strong and he managed almost three-quarters of a mile. The house he sought must have been within his vision when he died, for we could see it quite clearly when we came to his body by the roadside. His eyes were open and his tongue was clenched between his teeth and the little blood he had left dropped red and black on the winter snow. He was not to be saved for a future time anymore.

I learned later that my father had asked the neighbour to shoot him and that we had led him into a kind of ambush. Perhaps my father did so because the neighbour was younger and had a better gun or was a better shot. Perhaps because my father did not want to be involved. It was obvious he had not planned on things turning out so messy.

The dog had become increasingly powerful and protective to the extent that people were afraid to come into our yard. And he had also bitten two of the neighbour's children and caused them to be frightened of passing our house on their journeys to and from school.

And perhaps there was also the feeling in the community that he was getting more than his share of the breeding: that he travelled farther than other dog on his nightly forays and that he fought off and injured the smaller dogs who might compete with him for female favours. Perhaps there was fear that his dominance and undesirable characteristics did not bode well for future generations.

This has been the writing down of a memory triggered by the sight of a golden dog at play in the silent snow with my own excited children. After they came in and had their hot chocolate, the wind began to blow. By the time I left for work, there was no evidence of their early-morning revels or any dog tracks leading to the chain-link fence. The "enclosed" dog looked impassively at me as I brushed the snow from the buried windshield. *What does he know?* he seemed to say.

The snow continues to drift and to persist as another uncertainty added to those we already have. Should we be forced to drive tonight, it will be a long, tough journey into the wind and the driving snow, which is pounding across Ontario, Quebec, and New Brunswick, and against the granite coast of Nova Scotia. Should we be drawn by death, we might well meet our own. Still, it is only because I am alive that I can even consider such possibilities. Had I not been saved by the golden dog, I would not have these tight concerns or children playing in the snow or, of course, these memories. It is because of him that I have been able to come this far.

It is too bad that I could not have saved him as well. My feelings did him little good as I looked upon his bloodied body there beside the road. It was too late and out of my control and if I had known the possibilities of the future it would not have been easy.

He was with us only a short while and brought his own changes, and yet he still persists. He persists in my memory and in my life and he persists physically as well. He is there in this winter storm. There in the golden-grey dogs with their black-tipped ears and tail, sleeping in the stables or in the lees of woodpiles or under porches or curled beside the houses which face towards the sea.

SQUARE BEAM
A. R. Scammell

A true experience of Skipper Ned Hynes of Change Islands, Newfoundland, as told to A. R. Scammell.

kipper Ned Hynes, a veteran of the First World War, rowing hard in the bow of his gunning punt, saw the after paddles go slack and the body of his nephew, Ralph King, slump to the bottom of the boat. He had known for some time that the lad was giving out under the hard strain. His heart wasn't too strong.

They had left their home on Change Islands early that morning—February 8, 1949—to hunt sea-ducks at Duck Island, about three miles away. It had been fairly calm then and they had followed the standing edge of ice which extended up to the Shag Rocks and from there to their intended goal.

Hauling up the punt on the east end of Duck Island, they had shot nine ducks in two hours. The wind then freshened to about forty miles an hour and was still rising with blinding snow, so they decided to leave for home.

"The wind shouldn't bother us much," Ned had told Ralph. "The firm ice is to the wind'ard of us and that'll keep the water smooth."

They had rowed for about an hour. Then the snowstorm cleared and, to their surprise, they found themselves two miles to the leeward of their destination, Gannets Island Point. The firm ice in the run had broken up under the force of the wind and they had been rowing along a moving ice edge instead of a standing one. Snow had prevented them from seeing this.

Skipper Ned had to adjust his thinking to the new situation. His old antagonists, sea wind and ice, were up to their tricks again, testing his nerve and ingenuity.

"The best thing we can do, boy," he said, "is run back toward Herring Neck by the edge of the ice. Change Islands is cut off from us."

"Okay, Uncle Ned. We can buck that," replied Ralph.

In his heart Ned had doubts, and an hour's hard rowing only confirmed his fears. That was when Ralph gave out and Ned realized that whatever he did, he would have to do alone. His plan of reaching Herring Neck would have to be given up, for his long experience had taught him the uselessness of pitting man's puny physical strength against the tireless, giant forces of nature. Only human wit and nerve were of any use.

His only chance now was to try and reach Baccalieu, a large high island further leeward. It was uninhabited in winter, Ned knew, but it had a lighthouse and also some seal hunter's shacks. But the ice was striking in on that island too, and he knew he'd have his work cut out for him to reach it by dark.

Entering the ice, he poked and launched over it and through it. Progress was slow—painfully slow. The punt, with its burden of death, got no lighter with the dragging hours; only the man, working desperately, felt the passage of time. And time was precious, the February days short. Ned knew he had to get to land and shelter before night fell or Rhoda, his wife, would be a widow.

Standing on the punt's thwart, Ned could just see black water on the other side of the ice outside the island. That gave him hope. Where there was water he could at least use his paddles to make better speed. When he reached the water, he was three miles outside of Baccalieu. The wind had died down, relenting in the face of human courage. Ned shipped out his paddles and began his long row to the island.

The occasional flock of ducks passed on swift, mocking wings, disdaining even to fly out of range of an insignificant human, paddling tortoise slow. Somehow Ned drew strength from their flight. The same life force propelling them was pulsing along his own veins, and would pulse 'til that black water two feet below his thole pin stopped it forever.

He knew Rhoda would be nearly frantic by this time. For a moment he allowed himself the luxury of thinking of her concern. Then his glance flickered to the corpse beside him. One dead and one alive. The scales were even so far. Would the balance hold? *Square beam*, thought Ned wryly, his mind fastening on a local phrase that the fishery men used when weighing off their salt cod in the merchant's storage shed.

The fight was not over yet—not by a long shot. Darkness had fallen when Ned reached a little cove on Baccalieu, called Seal Harbour Low. His first concern was for the dead man. Wearily, arms dragging, clothes saturated with saltwater spray, he hauled the inert body out of the boat and up onto the snow.

Next he had to try and save the punt. A lifeless thing of wood, nails, and paint, she had become more than that in her owner's mind—the obedient silent partner in his fight for life. She, too, deserved to be saved. Up the straight wall of ballicater ice she had to come. Ned struggled and scooted 'til he had her safe on the level snow. He threw himself panting across her for a moment, letting his heart regain a more normal rhythm.

Walking about a mile, he came to the hunting shelters where he found food, wood, and bedding. A fire was next on the program and, after a time, he discovered a small box with two matches. His own were soaked. The first didn't light. With a muttered curse on the manufacturers, Ned found a lamp before he tried the second one and hurriedly transferred the tiny flame to the steady reliable wick. He then ate his first bite of the day. His tobacco was wet, so he couldn't get a smoke but there would be time now for many future draws, please God.

The wind had veered to the northwest, a gale, and before he lay down, he walked over to the punt to see if he could get her in around to the leeward side of the island. It was not possible.

He didn't sleep much that night. For one thing, the stovepipe blew off three or four times and he had to get out and fix it, finally nailing it on with the axe. For another thing, the stretched tension of the day's events, the death of his nephew, and his own exertions would take more than one night to dispel.

Next morning the wind had abated. He walked across the island, covered up Ralph's corpse, brought back a duck to cook and dried out his tobacco in an enamel pan over the stove. Then he went to the lighthouse with a rug, climbed up the lineless flagpole and tied it on, hoping to attract attention from either Herring Neck or Change Islands.

Shortly afterward the same day, he heard the welcome *putt-putt* of a motorboat. It was Charlie Watton and eight other men from his home town. Knowing Ned, they were not surprised to find him alive, but they were amazed that one man could, singlehandedly, get the punt where she was. The next port of call was home and Rhoda.

For two weeks thereafter, after proving once more his manhood against the elements, Ned had to stay in the house wearing napkins like a baby. His strenuous exertions had chafed him raw-beef sore in all parts of the human anatomy where napkins give protection.

ONE SPECIAL PRESENT
Michael Nowlan

*M*ickey Rice wanted skates for Christmas. Mickey, however, was fussy. He did not want just any skates. He wanted Tower Supremes. He often thought of gliding through centre ice, shifting…now left…now right…as he approached the opponent's blue line. From here, it would be a mere dash to the goal on such a sturdy pair of skates.

Mickey looked back on the last five Christmases.

"Look at all that stuff they bought me: things they thought I wanted. Oh, yes, I liked it all, but they never seem to listen to what I really want. This Christmas will be the same," he said disgustedly.

He spoke to no one in particular because he was babysitting his younger brother who was already asleep.

"Don't Dad and Mom remember Christmas when they were kids?" he exclaimed. With that, he kicked at a cushion on the floor by the couch.

He dreamed of Christmas morning with the tree, the candy, the wonderful things his mother baked—and the presents. His mind drifted to the big box so nicely wrapped and he knew it had to contain skates. Again he saw himself plunging toward the goalmouth in a championship game.

Although this was only a dream, Mickey Rice was a determined boy for fourteen. He would get those skates for Christmas. He would make it plain that was all he wanted. He knew, nevertheless, it would take solid persuasion to get his father to buy Tower Supremes.

Mr. Rice was certain Mickey did not need such an expensive pair of skates. He knew Mickey skated and performed well in all his hockey games. In fact, Mickey was one of his team's leading scorers. When Mickey made the all-star rep team for the first time, he was only ten years old. He loved the game and, like so many hockey-playing kids, dreamed of the day he would play for an NHL team. In Mickey's case, that team would be his beloved Montreal Canadiens.

Perhaps it was the fun Mickey got from hockey that was so important. Since he was an exceptionally strong skater, he could often break away to score goals. The sense of power thrilled him. To hit a winger with a perfect pass also excited him as a teammate scored. All this would be so much easier with Supremes.

To get that skate package under the tree on Christmas morning needed a very definite scheme. Mickey decided, "A quiet campaign to convince Dad will be best. I'll make one simple request for one special present this year. I'll even forego all the candy and stocking stuff." He was satisfied with his plan.

The next morning at breakfast, Mickey eagerly approached the subject.

"Dad, this year for Christmas I want only one thing."

Mr. Rice glanced up from his bacon and eggs and, with a mouth half-full of toast, muttered, "Yeah, what's that?"

Mickey hesitated. "Dad, I want a pair of Tower Supremes. *Please*!"

Mr. Rice put down his fork, took a drink of coffee, and stared briefly at Mickey. Then he shook his head slowly. "No, Mickey; I've told you before you don't need them. Besides, your mother and I have other ideas in mind for Christmas."

"You're joking," snapped Mickey.

But Mickey said no more. Half-heartedly, he finished his breakfast. Since it was Saturday, he slipped off to his room where he would be alone.

Why? Why does it have to be like this? he wondered. To try another tactic or to plead would only annoy his father, and he knew what that meant. He sat motionless, staring blankly at the trophies, pictures, and posters around his room. After a moment, he saw the mail-order catalogue which was open at the skate page. A large, colourful illustration of the Tower Supremes was there before him. Mickey brightened. He jumped up and picked up the catalogue. "From now until Christmas, I'll leave magazines and catalogues open at Tower Supreme skate pages. I'll put them where Dad will be sure to see them," he said to himself.

Toward the end of November, Mickey began to think seriously about Christmas. The upcoming tree, presents, and lights tantalized him. "But what about the Tower Supremes?" he said aloud one day as he walked home from school. "I'm sure Dad did not get them yet." He had left many hints, but he had never talked about the Supremes since that morning back in October. He even saw his father reading one of the advertisements very carefully.

He knew his mother was buying presents. He always noticed when parcels were rushed off to his parents' bedroom. It was time to start his annual snooping.

The next time Mickey babysat was the middle of December. After his brother went to sleep, Mickey searched for Christmas gifts. Sure enough, they were there. All kinds of them. Even things for stockings. Some of the packages were brightly wrapped, so he could not see what was in them. They had come by mail from relatives. Sadly, there were no skates. Actually, there was no "big" gift for Mickey.

Maybe there would be skates. What were those other ideas they had?

"Dad is always so mysterious," he mused. "I'll bet they were going to get skates after all," he concluded, but not very convincingly. On the other hand, if they were not getting skates, why was there not something else for him among all the things he saw?

From then on, Mickey spied as much as he could each day. He knew his father would have to travel to the city to get the skates. That was twenty miles away. He started checking the odometer on the car. Each day it would show only enough mileage to get his father back and forth to work; or to go to the shopping plaza, which did not sell Supremes.

He watched for the mailman and delivery trucks. Nothing came.

"Dad and Mom wouldn't leave me out at Christmas, would they? Perhaps I used too many hints. Maybe they're mad at me," he whimpered as he tried to sleep three nights before Christmas.

The next day, Mickey looked at the odometer again.

He asked his mother: "Did Dad go anywhere with someone else this week?"

"Why no, Michael, not to my knowledge. Why?" His mother still called him Michael even though everyone else used Mickey, a nickname he had picked up at hockey school three summers before.

"Oh, I was just wondering," Mickey let the questions drop.

Christmas Eve came. He was certain there was no gift for him. Something was wrong. What was Christmas going to be like? He was sick at the thought of it.

After lunch, he said, "Dad, are you going to the city this afternoon?"

"No, son. We have everything we need…I hope." Mr. Rice was never sure they had everything at Christmas.

The day passed into evening and all the coloured lights shone brightly along Lark Street. Mickey looked out at them but did not feel the spirit of the season. Not only were there no skates, there was nothing. During the day his mother had placed numerous gifts under the tree, but there was no big package marked *TO MICKEY — FROM MOM AND DAD*. There was something for everyone else in the family.

When bedtime came, Mickey went off to his room, convinced he had done something terrible through all his hints with magazines, catalogues, and pictures of Tower Supremes.

"Why did I do it?" he said over and over before he finally slept.

As Christmas Eve night settled over the community, the tree in the Rice home sparkled. Under it was one of the most special presents Mickey Rice would ever open on Christmas morning.

With expectancy, but more than a little uncertainty, Mickey came downstairs the next morning. The stockings were bulging as usual. His little brother was tearing paper from two packages at once. The others were looking for gifts with the right name.

It was then that Mickey saw it. That one special present. It was there.

The Supremes!

It was truly Christmas.

He carefully removed the bright red paper. He opened the box and stared at the beautiful leather, the shiny blades. He said nothing, but sure loved his "mysterious" Dad at that moment.

Mickey's expression caused his father to remark, "After you children were asleep, I went over to see Fred who picked up the Supremes for me in the city two weeks ago."

THE LUNENBURG WAY
Archibald MacMechan

The four-masted schooner *Joan Keilberg* was lying alongside the grimy wharf, having just made Halifax in seventy hours from Flushing, New York, with a load of coal. Her captain, "Jimmy Leander" Publicover, knows how to get the most out of his handsome, speedy, nine-hundred-ton vessel. Five men out of Lunenburg suffice to handle her. His father, Leander, Mark I, aged seventy-six, sails with him as mate, and gave a hint how the *Joan Keilberg* earned profits for her owners in the lean years, when she carried pulpwood summer and winter, in all weathers, from Mahone Bay to New York.

"Been sailin' two years and never tied a reef p'int in her yet. May have eased the peak-halliards," he conceded.

Captain Publicover was discovered in his ample cabin making a toy schooner. Mrs. Publicover was entertaining friends. Several children were playing about but Billy, the eldest, aged sixteen, was living in the fo'c's'l, learning his trade like his father and his grandfather before him. Captain Publicover is a little, slight, dark, neat-footed man with a high arched aquiline nose. His expression is close, unsmiling, suggestive of nerves and anxieties. He could not be described as a willing witness, when he told of his experience with the water-logged *Tilton*. The facts had rather to be dragged out of him. One would almost think the gold watch and chain awarded him officially by President Woodrow Wilson in the name of Great

Republic for saving the lives of seven American soldiers involved some sort of scandal. But the Lunenburg way is not effusive.

In December 1912, Captain Publicover was bringing the tern schooner *W. N. Zwicker*, of 398 tons, back from New York to Ingram Docks in Nova Scotia. His brother Charles, aged eighteen, was mate, with three years experience; and the other seven were all Lunenburg boys of the finest race of sailors afloat. On Friday, the 20, the *Zwicker* was forty miles east-northeast of Cape Cod, homeward bound in a gale from the northwest with snow squalls and a heavy sea. It was typical North Atlantic winter weather. She was proceeding with reduced canvas, reefed mainsail, foresail, and staysail; the big spanker was safely stowed, as well as the jibs. At Flushing, the *Zwicker* had been swept clean and was navigating without an ounce of cargo or ballast. Most expert handling was needed to keep her from turning over.

"At 9 A.M.," said Captain Publicover, "I sighted a tern schooner flying signals of distress, about two points off our lee bow and four or five miles away. She was heading south. She appeared as if hove-to but, through the glass, I could see the gaffs. Her sails were blown away. I swung my vessel off and bore right down on her.

"We did not dare to go close enough to hail, but we could see seven men lashed to the spanker boom over the cabin house, one after the other. They were sitting in the lee, of course, and got a little shelter from the waves, which were breaking over her constantly.

"The decks were all that much under water." and he held his hand about four feet above the cabin floor. "Only the high bowsprit and the gaff were showing. The sea was breaking like over a ledge, and it was bitter cold."

A vessel with her decks under water, either waterlogged or sinking, looks like a living person being lowered into an open grave. This was the plight of the tern schooner, *Henry B. Tilton* of Isleboro, Maine, with P. W. Sprague as master. Thirty-six years old, she had left Windsor, Nova Scotia, lumber-laden, for New York a few days before, but had encountered heavy gales. Her sails had been blown away, her seams had opened and let in the sea 'til she was waterlogged, her bulwarks smashed, her boats gone, her stern stove in, and her whole deck load canted forward. Every wave, as it encountered the solid mass of the submerged hull, broke and burst in a sheet of foam as high as the three mastheads. The crew could do nothing more but await death or rescue. Every wave buried and half drowned them; and the smothering agony was momently renewed.

The problem Captain Publicover had to solve was by no means easy. Rendering assistance and saving life at sea come as natural to the sailor as breathing. But vessels have been known to sail away and leave shipwrecked men to their fate, like the stranger who abandoned the raft of the *Regina*. Publicover had been wrecked himself, and saving life was nothing new to him. When the *Virginia* piled up under the cliffs of LaHave at night, in the worst snowstorm in sixty years, he swung all his crew ashore, one after the other, over the bow, with the jib downhaul. He was willing enough to attempt the rescue. But there were other considerations.

It was wild weather. The steamer *Florence* was lost that day; the big liners were delayed and reported "the heaviest gales for years." Was he justified in risking his own vessel with all on board? She was light and rolled terribly. It seemed as if she might turn bottom up at every roll. Only the smartest handling could keep her from capsizing. Nor could she come near the wreck, or launch a boat. Publicover might lose his vessel, his crew, his own life, in a vain attempt at rescue. For hours he laboured for a decision, torn this way and that.

"I reached to the northward, until twelve o'clock," said Captain Publicover, "so as to get away from the schooner, and waited for the weather to moderate. If she sailed away, or drifted away, my conscience would be clear."

The seven frostbitten, half-drowned men, lashed to long boom, saw the strange sail come near enough to understand their desperate plight and then—desert them. Away she went to the northward 'til she was only an uncertain blur between the tumbling crested billows and the grey low-lying clouds. Their hearts died within them.

Then Publicover made up his mind. He wore ship, lowering his peaks, and came about.

"I set the jib and came back quick. About three o'clock we came up with her again. I was going to try to take off those men, but nobody on board expected me to get through with it.

"I got my dory on the poop with tackles in the rigging to get her over quick. A life buoy, an iron bucket for bailing, and the oars were lashed into her. When all was ready, I brought the schooner under the lee of the *Tilton*. I had to take chances every way, so I took 'em that way to start with. The sails were hauled down, and the wheel was hove hard down and lashed. I gave orders to the mate not to change her position unless I got to the leeward with the dory, in which case he was to run to the leeward of me and heave-to, which didn't happen.

"Then I called for a volunteer, because a ship master may not legally order a sailor to almost certain death, even if he himself leads the way.

"More than one came forward. Practically all. I picked Fred Richard, and made him understand if he drowned, my family wasn't to be blamed. I expected to be drowned myself."

That a captain should go off in a boat and leave his vessel in charge of the mate is clean against the ancient custom of the sea. It is unusual, almost unheard of. The captain's place is always aboard his ship. Publicover was criticized for this action, but it is hard to see what else he could have done.

Fred Richard, aged twenty, new to the coasting trade, and ignorant of danger, "jumped quick at the chance."

The two men stripped to their overalls and singlets, with their sheath knives in their belts. They stood in the thirteen-foot dory as she hung in the tackles, steadying themselves by lifelines rigged over the side. Then as their cockleshell dropped into the turmoil of the waves, on the weather side the two, with the swift precision of acrobats, unhooked the tackles, slashed the rope-yam that held the oars, and began to pull like madmen away from the *Zwicker*.

"That was the hardest part," said Captain Publicover.

They had to fight their way to windward over a quarter of a mile to the submerged hull of the *Tilton*.

"I called to the captain, and told him I would try and save him if he would obey my orders. Which he was very glad to do. I told him to unlash one man at a time and get him down in the lee mizzen rigging.

"So he did. It was smooth to leeward. We took two off the first time, one in each end of the boat. We drifted back about half a mile, but we daren't go alongside. They threw us lifelines from the schooner which we fastened round our passengers, and they hauled them on board same as a codfish."

For the first time, a faint smile crossed the captain's face.

"Our fellows boused them on, same as you'd haul a shark. The cook had hot coffee for them as soon as they got on the deck.

"That first trip we were almost lost under the counter. They took the man out of the stern first and almost swamped us. But that learned us."

Then they set out on their second strenuous pull to windward, a longer pull, for the vessels were always drifting farther apart, and took off two more men. Four men in a thirteen-foot dory would bring her gunwale very near the water; there was urgent need for the bailing bucket but somehow this miracle of rescue was performed a second time. A dory will live when a schooner will founder.

Then for the third time, in the failing light of the shortest day in the year but one, Publicover and Richard rowed back to the wreck and took off the three remaining men. Captain Sprague, of course, was the last to leave his vessel. If four men was a full load for the dory, five seemed impossible; but Lunenburg boys know how to handle a dory, so these two brought their precious freight to the safety of the rolling *Zwicker*.

"Then I said to Fred to send the bucket and life buoy and his oars and the thort on board. So he did. And we lost nothing. 'Now, Fred,' I said. 'You go in the lifeline.' The boys were getting anxious, for they didn't want me to go, and they thought they couldn't find the land without me.

"I watched for a good smooth. I made the end of one of the lifelines fast to the painter of the dory. The other I threw over my shoulder and grabbed my oars and the thort. By this time the dory was filled, and I was going up the side. We hoisted the dory in by one of the tackles, and the water spilled out of her. We lost nothing."

He was sweating in his overalls and singlet.

Expansiveness, as already noted, is not the Lunenburg way, but thrift is. There was no reason why a careful shipmaster who had earned the Victoria Cross three times in two hours should lose any of his gear—it costs money, and money is not easy to get in the coasting trade. After saving the crew of the *Tilton*, Publicover's mind turned not to thoughts of fame or self-congratulation, but to saving his dory and everything in it down to the movable thwarts. His strongest feeling must have been thankfulness to find the deck of the *Zwicker* under his feet once more.

"At eight o'clock we made sail and shaped our course for Seal Island, which we reached at four A.M."

By six o'clock that same evening, the *Zwicker* had beat into the majestic entrance of the La Have River and anchored with twenty fathom of chain. That closed the episode as far as Captain Publicover was concerned. Of course, he logged the incident in the "Remarks" for December 20 as the law requires, without waste of words or undue display of emotion. The entry reads, in part: *This day comes in blowing a gale of wind and a heavy sea running, put out a boat and rescued the crew of a distress vessel, it being very dangerous work.*

But Captain Publicover was not allowed to be the grave of his own deserving. Captain Sprague was passed up the river, with his men, to the care of the American consular agent at Bridgewater. No seal was on his lips, and he put the whole affair in a different light, when he made his official report to Mr. S. A. Chesley.

"Although in the face of the storm and terrible seas then prevailing the attempt seemed perfect folly,"

Publicover and Richard did, in fact, what they set out to do.

"The dangers of the transference," continues Captain Sprague, "were almost indescribable, and the heroism of the two men who accomplished it beyond praise."

Five months later, at Mr. Chesley's instance, Captain Publicover made a sworn statement of the facts as related before him, and attested a copy of the entries in the log. Mr. Chesley, in turn, made representations to the American Consul at Lunenburg. And, in the end, the Lunenburg captain got his watch from President Wilson, and Fred Richard a gold medal, with an inscription on one side, and a woman's head on the other, "in recognition of his heroic services."

WHEN THE REINDEER CAME
TO NEWFOUNDLAND

Michael Francis Harrington

*T*here is a distinct possibility that one of Santa's reindeer is a Newfoundland caribou. Prancer, Cupid, Dancer, or Vixen—any one of the eight could have caribou blood in their veins. For, basically, reindeer and caribou are the same animal, and although reindeer are not indigenous to Newfoundland, there were real reindeer in the province half a century ago.

How did this happen? The great medical missionary pioneer, Dr. Wilfred Grenfell, was responsible. In 1907, Grenfell read about the success of an American experiment that introduced reindeer into Alaska for the benefit of the Inuit. The inspiration behind the Alaskan venture had been Dr. Sheldon Jackson, a medical missionary like Grenfell, who had started his experiment in 1891, just at the time when Grenfell made his appearance on the Newfoundland scene. Grenfell went to Washington, DC, to confer with Jackson, and returned to Newfoundland convinced the same thing could be done for the Inuit of Labrador.

Reindeer are tame, hardy animals that provide milk and meat for food, fur and leather for clothing, and are invaluable in many folk industries. The reindeer is also extremely valuable in the field of transport, which accounts for its traditional significance in the Christmas itinerary of St. Nicholas. The transportation factor appealed to the Anglo-Newfoundland Development Company which was then in the process of building its paper mill at Grand Falls. They agreed to take fifty animals, which would be employed in wood-hauling operations.

Grenfell arranged for a shipment of three hundred animals, which left Lapland on December 30, 1907. Their destination was the Grenfell Mission headquarters at St. Anthony at the northern tip of Newfoundland. The animals were accompanied by Lapp herdsmen and their families. The ship arrived off St. Anthony on January 20, 1908, but could not enter because of a barrier of slob ice extending eight miles offshore. The decision was made to lower the reindeer into the sea and let them make their own way to land.

The herdsmen went ashore over the ice to wait for the animals. As each clambered ashore it was either tethered or turned loose with a string of bells around its neck. Some of them, instead of making for land through the slob ice, turned and swam out to sea and out of sight. Nevertheless, and this in itself is a remarkable incident, all three hundred reindeer were eventually accounted for by the waiting Lapps.

Dr. Grenfell had his reindeer ashore, but fifty of them belonged to the A. N. D. Company, destined for the logging areas near the railway junction of Millertown. It was decided to drive them there at once. Hugh Cole, a stocky young Englishman who had joined the company's survey department in 1905, and had already proven his resourcefulness and endurance, was given the job. (Cole died in St. John's at the age of seventy-six in 1960.)

Cole, and a lone companion, Tom Greening, a woods foreman, took the train to Deer Lake on January 25, 1908. They had a dog team, a camping outfit, and a week's grub. They put on snowshoes at Deer Lake and hardly took them off again until they returned to Millertown after a three-month, thousand-mile journey in what turned out to be the hardest winter for many years. They were a whole week getting to Bonne Bay, where they were joined by a famous Mi'kmaw guide, Mattie Mitchell.

Now they started up the St. Barbe Coast, reaching Hawke Bay a day later. Here they engaged a local guide and struck across the long, finger-like peninsula ("Petit Nord," the French called it) to come out at Canada Bay. It was February 15 and they just managed to reach shelter before a blizzard broke, followed by heavy rain. Crossing Canada Bay on the ice, they took the trail to Hare Bay, crossed it, and were storm-stayed a second time in a deserted house. Eighteen days after leaving Deer Lake they plodded into St. Anthony.

The Lapland reindeer had been there more than a month and were in poor condition. The supply of Lapland moss, brought out to feed them, was gone; deep snow covered the sphagnum moss, and even the sharp hooves of the animals could not get through the covering of snow and ice. This situation persisted during the trek, but Cole and his men were able to feed the herd on the "moll-dow" growing on the spruce trees. At St. Anthony they were joined by Morris Sundine, a second-generation member of one of the Swedish families brought to Newfoundland by the Scottish lumberman, Lewis Miller. Millertown and Lewisporte are called after him.

Sundine, who spoke Swedish, was to be the interpreter for the Lapps. There were five of them: Aslec Sombie, sixty-four; his wife, sixty-three; Pere Sombie, thirty-eight; his wife, Maretta; and their son. Maretta was a deaf-mute, but her ability to read sign language was a help rather than a hindrance.

On March 3, 1908, the expedition left St. Anthony—six men, two women, ten dogs, and fifty reindeer. Forty of these were does heavy with fawn. There were four stags, six hauling-stags, and four reindeer-herding dogs. The women rode in *pulkas*, Lapp sleds. They had four with them. The normal route should have led across the ice of Hare and Canada Bays, down the east coast, across the ice in Sop's Arm, then via Hampden in White Bay to Sandy Lake and Kitty's Brook, and down the Hind's Valley to Millertown. But this trail had to be abandoned because the ice in the bays, lakes, and large rivers was too smooth. The reindeer could not walk on it without falling. So the party had to take to the high, barren country, the spine of the peninsula (average height two thousand feet) where the altitude meant exceptional cold, snow, and hardship.

Other troubles were soon added. The reindeer were inclined to wander, and the tendency was to return to the main herd at St. Anthony. Then, above all things, the Lapps went snow-blind. In spite of these setbacks, the expedition managed to average thirteen miles a day in wretched weather. There were no accidents, except when one of the hauling stags was bitten by a sled dog.

Hugh Cole kept a diary of the journey. A typical entry reveals the trying nature of the expedition, especially when they ran short of food. Mitchell and Greening were sent back to Sop's Arm for supplies on Sunday, March 29. The men had barely enough rice for three meals, eight pounds of meat and a half-pound of tea. Three days passed and April came with a high wind from the south. The temperature soared to thirty-five degrees, but there was no sign of Greening or the Mi'kmaw guide. With only a day's rations left, Cole became worried, and grew even more anxious when Thursday came with gales, snow and sub-zero temperatures.

This weather continued through Friday and Saturday, with the party on one meal a day, tea twice-boiled, after which they dried the leaves and smoked them. It was so stormy Friday night they thought their tent would blow way. It was full of snow by morning and their stove had collapsed. They went out, however, and marked the trail from the camp to the brook in case the others returned. But it was too bad a day for the party to face the brook, which was buried by snowdrifts.

A week had passed since Greening and Mitchell went to Sop's Arm. Cole had begun to give up hope of ever seeing them again. Cole told Sundine to tell the Lapps that eating meat before they slept was a bad practice. But they all looked so sad he gave them the last pound. It seemed as if they would have to kill one of the reindeer, but it would be a last resort.

Monday, April 6, was a fine morning. They rose early, cooked breakfast, and had the herd rounded up by half-past six. They were just about to move on when they heard gunshots. Next, Tom Greening and five other men came out of the woods with packs on their backs. Two hours later Mitchell and two other men arrived with a second load. The account each group gave of their hardship and adventures is a story in itself.

Now that the expedition had been reunited and supplied with provisions, it was wisely decided to abandon the southward route to Deer Lake and retrace the trail they had followed on the way to St. Anthony. On this stage of the journey one of the does disappeared—the only loss the herd suffered during the entire operation. By April 11 the expedition was at the two-thousand-foot line of the Long Range Mountains and it took them five days to find a way down to the St. Lawrence foreshore in an almost continuous snowstorm.

The snow kept falling while they made their way along the coast to Bonne Bay, while the reindeer swam St. Paul's Inlet. Bonne Bay was reached on April 19. Deer Lake, four days later. Here, Cole and some of the party took the train to Millertown to prepare for the reception of the herd, while the others escorted the reindeer overland. The herd reached its destination around April 30 and was located in a permanent "camp" on Marcy March River.

The expedition had been a notable success for the leader and his assistants. No (human) lives had been lost, there had been no accidents, and losses to the herd were limited to the doe that went astray and the stag with the injured leg. In the end, the stag had to be shot. The herd and the Lapp herdsmen were more or less on exhibition for the next few months. The herd increased by fifty percent when does gave birth to twenty-five fawns, with neither mothers nor babies being any the worse for the long journey.

But the great Newfoundland reindeer trek of the winter of 1908 ended in disappointment. After all the trouble to get them there, it was quickly found that the reindeer could not be used by the A. N. D. Company. The Red Indian Lake area did not produce enough moss, grass, and leaves to support the herd, and it was regretfully decided to send them back to St. Anthony. This time the reindeer travelled by schooner.

Dr. Grenfell got the best of the bargain. He sent the company 50 reindeer and got back 73. In the meantime the St. Anthony herd had increased to 481 with the addition of another 160 fawns. From there on, however, tragedy dogged the reindeer. Men shot them and dogs dragged them down, while the government made no move to protect them. Finally, in 1919, Grenfell, in disgust, gathered together those remaining and turned them loose in Labrador.

The record is silent on their fate thereafter.

THE ICE RUN
Tom Pond

It had been a winter of heavy ice in the Miramichi River. Cold weather during December and early January before the big snowstorms came, had resulted in a deep freeze. By the time the warm sunshine of April started the thaw, even the rapids in the river were frozen over thickly enough to carry a team of horses.

Old-timers differed in opinion as to how this would affect the ice run. There were, of course, the prophets of doom, who forecast heavy rains, which would cause early flooding to break up the ice before it could melt away. This heavy ice, they said, would tear out bridges and damage riverbanks. The jams were bound to tear up and destroy the salmon spawning beds on the shallow bars.

There were others of equal authority who pointed out that the same conditions had existed in previous years, but a long period of warm sunny weather during the spring thaw had resulted in the ice wasting away, so that when it did run it was only slush and did very little, if any, damage.

The boys in my group, who looked forward to watching the ice go out, secretly favored the predictions of the prophets of doom, for they seemed to have a much more interesting way of ending the long winter. At recess we would gather at the sunny end of the schoolhouse to exchange information on ice conditions and plan our strategy for a get-together at a carefully chosen lookout point to watch the event. Girls and small boys were not allowed at these bull sessions, and they soon learned that there was a snowball hazard for those who tried. They could not be trusted to keep secrets, and a teacher or parents forewarned could interfere with jigging school on short notice if that became necessary.

The weather held fine and warm through the first half of April with very little rain to speak of, but the snow was now melting fast in the fields and on the south slopes; small brooks were open and starting to flood but the river ice, although lifted along the shores, was holding solid. The time was ripe and a heavy rain was long past due.

On Thursday in the third week of April it came. It was no ordinary spring shower, but a steady downpour Thursday night and Friday. The small brooks were raging torrents and there was heavy runoff everywhere. Saturday dawned bright and sunny, and by eight-thirty every boy of age was on the muddy settlement road, headed for the river. A few of the older boys rode horseback with a bag of hay feed serving as a saddle, but most of us walked in groups, picking up friends along the way. There was little dilly-dallying for we knew this was the zero hour. Each boy had a lunch, usually tied up in a clean big handkerchief and fastened to his belt or braces, for it might be well into the late afternoon before the show was over.

There were patches of deep snow in the thick stands of fir, spruce and pine along the old logging road leading from the highway to the river, but the cleared space at the top of the old log landing site on the high riverbank was bare. Two of the boys had brought axes so we soon had a pile of wood dragged out from the woods nearby and a fire going. We did not need this for its warmth, for it was bright and sunny here in this sheltered place, but there's nothing like a good open fire to sit by when you are waiting for something to happen.

There were about a dozen boys in our group and although some grew impatient with waiting, time passed quickly until noon—many fertile minds plus a little spring fever means there is bound to be action of some kind. Even the "gorbies," or moose birds as they are sometimes called, drawn to this spot by the smoke from our fire, seemed to have a spirit of anticipation, but perhaps for a different reason. To them, smoke meant a lunch fire and handouts. Champion scroungers of the wilds, they seemed to be able to smell a lunch fire for miles. Every lumberjack's lunching hole had its devoted attendance.

Many lumberjacks believed that woodsmen who departed this life for the beyond eventually came back in the form of a gorbie, and it was woe and bad luck to harm one, even though it became so much of a nuisance that it would dart down and fly off with a piece of meat from your lunch. You might cuss him and even insult his ancestors if you recognized his origin, but he had to be tolerated. There were many stories of the fate of non-believers. One which I remember from my early and impressionable boyhood days, was of a non-gorbie-lover who being bothered at the lunch hole by a particularly offensive bird, caught it and pulled out its tail feathers. A year later he developed a heavy fever during which all his hair fell out, leaving him bald for the rest of his life. Out of respect for the wisdom of my elders, to this day I have never put this superstition to the test.

Gorbies, like people, have different characteristics: some are shy and cautious, others are bold; there are expert thieves and scroungers amongst them; bullies, noisy characters, and gluttons. While waiting by our fire we tried to identify the individual birds with some old-timer long gone, who we knew by reputation, while in the meantime we shared our lunch with them. One boy had a long string in his pocket, which he tied to a piece of meat from his lunch kit, and placed on a stick by the fire. He hardly had time to get back on his seat before old Henry, the bold one, dived down and took off with it in his beak. At the end of the string he went into a flip-flop but with a great flutter of wings managed to stay airborne until he reached a tree limb, where he sat for a few minutes preening his feathers back into shape and regaining his dignity. In the meantime, the meat had been again placed on the stick.

This time, however, Henry approached more cautiously, lighting on the end of the stick, he looked it over between hops, then suddenly pounced, grabbing it in his beak, but dropping it to catch it with his feet almost immediately. He didn't understand about strings. Old Henry was smart though, and it didn't take him long to figure out another way. Next time he ignored the hazards, hopped down, and started pecking at the meat where it lay. He was doing fine until the cautious ones looking on saw what a good thing he had and started dropping down to help him. After a short, noisy free-for-all, the meat came loose from the string and one of the newcomers flew away with it, the rest in hot pursuit.

By mid-afternoon some of the less patient boys had wandered off. At about three o'clock we heard a rumbling sound from upriver. We knew most of the upriver ice had run down to a place called "the Dungeon" which was about four miles above our lookout. Here, where the river narrowed between two steep ledges, a two-mile jam had formed. The noise we were now hearing sounded like a distant freight train.

The rumbling continued to increase and soon we could hear a loud snapping as the thick sheets of blue ice broke under pressure. When the head of this jam came into sight around the turn above us, it appeared like a great bulldozer rolling everything before it. As it crowded down, the entire sheet of ice in the pool before us started to move intact, where the space between the banks narrowed.

The edge of the big sheet shoved up on the shore to the tree line, moving boulders and torn-out clumps of bushes before it. Then, with a loud *crrrack* like a rifle shot, it split down the centre and began to break into smaller sections. Sometimes great sheets would be lifted up to stand on their edges before crashing down on the top of the jam, sending broken ice in all directions.

The din was terrific. Where only a few moments ago there was only the sound of our voices and the chirping of the gorbies, the valley was suddenly full of the sound of roaring water, of breaking and grinding ice. We almost had to shout to be heard.

As the main part of the jam reached our lookout, we could see old logs, bits of lumber, boulders, and the remains of one cottage— built too near the shore—mixed with the ice cakes. A large spruce tree torn from the bank, the frozen soil around its roots intact, stood almost upright as it was carried along, locked into this position by the packed ice around it. As this deeply packed mass of ice passed over the bar at the head of the pool, the bottom sheets gouged out rocks and gravel, lifting them up like a bulldozer.

A mile below us, where the river took a bend against a steep bank, the ice began to slide up and pile against the shore, narrowing the channel until another jam was formed. As the ice backed up to our lookout point, the pressure from behind continued to increase, and again the noise of grinding and breaking ice filled the valley with sound, for the new jam was now two or three miles long, completely blocking the channel. But the steady build up of water behind it had to find an outlet and soon it broke over the low banks of the intervale on the opposite shore.

It formed a new channel there, carrying great cakes of ice with it. This intervale had been cleared of trees for farming, but two giant elms—nearly three feet in diameter and seventy feet high—had been left standing. These were now directly in the path the ice was taking and soon the big cakes, travelling five to ten miles per hour, were crashing against the trees like battering rams. Each time a cake struck, the top of the tree shook. Soon the upper side of the trunk was bare of bark. Finally the tree directly in the run began to lean a little more and the cakes began sliding farther up on the trunk, jamming there. Under the added pressure the tree swayed crazily with each bump until finally it gave way and crashed down to be swallowed up in the ice jam, only a few great limbs showing as it was swept along in the current.

The intervale ended where the river turned against the high bank, so the channel across the intervale was blocked here and the ice it carried jammed against the ice in the main channel. But new ice continued to come in from the river above until it covered the intervale land.

In the main jam, all was quiet now or as quiet as an ice jam can be, there was still the roar of water trying to get around the ice cakes and an occasional grinding and breaking sound as the pressure increased, but the show was over for the time being. The horses were restless and tramping around and our stomachs suddenly reminded us that it was well past our feeding time too. Reluctantly we headed home, but all agreed to return early the next day in hopes of witnessing the final act in this great show of nature's might.

No one saw the ice jam break, for it went out during the night. People living a half mile away were awakened by the noise it made. But we kept our rendezvous the next day, for there was much to see of the wreckage.

Broad thick cakes of clear blue ice, weighing tons, were piled high on the sloping shores. Occasionally one of these great cakes moved and went sliding into the river to float away. The intervale was covered with ice piled at all angles, blue edges glistening in the sun. It would be very late in the planting season before these melted. Here and there the ice had gouged out the soil leaving big holes full of water, a new environment for frogs, nesting ducks, or muskrats. Out on the stranded ice cakes flocks of ravens and crows had found dead salmon and other fish. There were also muskrats, beaver, and other animals that had tarried too long in the path of the onrushing jam, and been ground to death in the churning mass.

Because this was the first time I witnessed this great demonstration of nature's power, I remember it well. Since then I have seen many floods and ice runs in mightier rivers. But this one was the beginning of my appreciation of what it must have been like in ancient times— when the raging torrents and massive cakes from receding glaciers tore out these great river valleys from the solid ledge in their race to the sea.

A WINTER'S TALE

Cassie Brown

he *Florizel* left the port of St. John's, Newfoundland, at 8 P.M. on Saturday, February 23, 1918, for Halifax and New York. About an hour or so later, a southeast gale and snowstorm came on and continued until midnight, when the wind chopped around to east-northeast, blowing with equal violence.

Aboard the *Florizel*, Captain William Martin was unworried. He had a sound ship, his equipment was good, and although it was a stormy night, she was capable of holding her own. Slob ice prevented the use of the log, which was the only accurate means of judging her speed. She was supposed to be making ten to twelve knots throughout the night and early hours of Sunday, but Captain Martin, allowing for wind, sea, and ice, estimated her speed at only six knots as a measure of precaution, so that when he ordered her course changed to south by west, he was sure he was well and safely out in the Atlantic, beyond Cape Race, and headed for Halifax. He was doubly confident since they had been steaming for nine hours on a six-hour leg.

One uneasy passenger who prowled restlessly around the ship that night was Captain Joe Kean, bound for Halifax to pick up a ship. He visited the captain on the bridge around 4 A.M. where they discussed the storm and the zero visibility, but he was apparently reassured by the captain's confidence.

It was so exciting. The last goodbyes had been said, relatives and boyfriends had been duly kissed and gone ashore, and the Red Cross

liner pulled slowly away from the wharf to midstream, preparatory
to departure for Halifax and New York.

Two young girls, Kitty Cantwell and Annie Dalton, linked arms
and strolled around to see what they could of the luxurious ship that
would be their home for the next week. Both girls were going to New
York: Annie to remain, Kitty to visit her married sister for a few weeks.

It was an unpleasant night, blowing and snowing even when the
Florizel pulled away from the wharf at eight o'clock, but the girls didn't
mind, they felt safe and snug inside the big liner.

In the course of their wanderings they ran into seaman William
Molloy, a young Newfoundlander who stayed at the home of Kitty's
aunt when he was ashore, and whom she knew quite well. He told
them, "You'd better get to your room; we're battening her down before
we get outside."

Duly warned, the girls went to their stateroom on the upper deck.
They were delighted with their room, which was spacious with
two berths, plenty of wardrobe space, and their own washroom. As
the *Florizel* steamed out of the Narrows on her last voyage, the two
young girls, who were old friends, chattered and giggled about their
boyfriends and set about hanging up their clothing.

Annie Dalton was pretty, vivacious, and popular. Her thick black
hair hung to her waist. Originally from Western Bay, Bay de Verde, she
had worked in St. John's long enough to become forewoman with the
British Clothing factory. She had been offered an even better position
with another clothing factory in New York, and the young girl seemed
to have a successful career ahead of her.

Kitty Cantwell, a blonde of twenty-three, was originally from
Torbay. She lived with her aunt on Parade Street, and had a boyfriend,
Mike McDonald, whom she was going to marry some day. But right
now she was looking forward to the excitement of the big city of New
York.

Their clothing hung and their luggage stowed, the girls prepared
for bed, unplaiting their hair, brushing and combing it vigorously,
before settling into their berths. It was quite stormy now—the ship

was tossing and rolling alarmingly—but it only added to Kitty's excitement.

Then Annie began to get sick. She was in the top berth and the constant pitch and roll of the ship began to take their toll. She turned a ghastly white and began to moan.

Kitty, chipper, and in top form on her first sea voyage, tried to cheer her friend. The captain, she reasoned, had taken the ship well out into the Atlantic in the storm and was letting her roll with the waves. She actually enjoyed the sensation. But Annie became worse, lying in her berth, quite helpless.

The storm worsened as the hours passed. Their luggage began to roll around in the stateroom; the clothing they had taken much care to hang danced wildly around and was flung to the floor. It was impossible to stand and try to bring any order to their room so Kitty, still excited and wide awake, lay in her berth, keeping up reassuring chatter for Annie.

She wasn't worried about the ship or the sea or the storm, but she was worried about Annie, who was too ill to throw up. Poor Annie was really suffering, and not a bit like herself.

Sometime during the night, Kitty heard the cheerful voice of a steward by the name of Gordon Ivany. He tapped on their door and came into their room. Knowing that this was their first voyage, he checked to see how they were faring. While there he pointed out to them the two lifebelts on the rack and told them how they should be used.

Young Minnie Denief was on her way to a new life in the United States that Saturday in February when she boarded the *Florizel*. Her plans were to join her sister, Mrs. Doerbecker, in New York, with whom she would live.

She was a thin girl with long black hair, and she wore heavy glasses because of her poor eyesight. Without them she was nearly blind. She was excited about the voyage as she waved goodbye to her family. She had already been settled into her second-class stateroom, and a young pantry steward on the *Florizel*, John Johnston, had promised her parents that he would keep a faithful eye on Minnie, and see that she would be all right during the trip.

As the liner moved midstream, Minnie met her stateroom companion, a Miss Pelley, who confided that she was going to live with a minister and his family. Then they both made friends with Mr. and Mrs. Mullowney, who had a stateroom next to theirs. The Mullowneys had a small baby. They chatted for a time, and the two young girls admitted that they had never been away from home before. Mullowney, an ex-serviceman just recovering from wounds received at Gallipoli, promised to take the two of them on a tour of the city of Halifax while the ship was docked there.

The weather worsened, and the ship was beginning to roll badly. Minnie and her companion, feeling a little sick, made a beeline for their stateroom, which was just off the saloon.

They unpacked hurriedly, for the ship was reeling and tossing wildly, and Minnie was downright seasick. Bed was the only place for them. Miss Pelley undressed completely and put on her nightdress, but Minnie was too ill to stand. She loosened her girdle, removed her dress, her long shoes, and stockings, and, keeping her slip and panties on, fell on her berth prostrate and violently ill.

Although seasick, Miss Pelley fell asleep, while Minnie lay there throughout the hours, convinced she was dying. Their stateroom was at the foot of the companionway that came down from the smoker and loud voices and laughter floated down, indicating that some people were enjoying themselves despite the bad weather. To add to her misery came the wailing of the Mullowneys' baby. The ship was reeling so that it was impossible to stand—not that she had any inclination to do so—and Minnie lay there, positive she would never last the night. Miss Pelley was sound asleep.

Harry Snow, a steward, tapped on their door to see how they were. He entered their room, saying: "It's a very bad night."

Minnie groaned. "I'm terribly sick. I'm dying," she said.

He joked: "Oh, come on now, no one ever dies on this ship."

With a few more words of encouragement he went out.

The *Florizel* was dangerously close to land and still well up the coast after the nine-hour run which should have taken her out into the Atlantic beyond Cape Race. When Captain Martin ordered the change in course, the bow of the *Florizel* pointed straight at the land, and within ten minutes she was hard and fast on Horn Head Point off Cappahayden on the southern shore of Newfoundland.

She struck amidships, listed to starboard, and immediately commenced to settle astern as the violent seas crashed in over her broadside. She struck with terrific force, the great rocks impaling her securely. Within seconds she was a wreck.

At first there was no great panic, although the seas were flooding in through the broken ship. Alex Ledingham, an engineer and first-class passenger, helped some steerage passengers into lifebelts when they came looking for them, then they all made their way fairly orderly to the companionway leading to the deck.

Many passengers had jammed the companionway with their luggage, all hoping, apparently, to make it to the lifeboats and quite unaware of the seriousness of the situation.

Harry Snow had barely left Minnie Denief's stateroom when there was a frightful grinding crash—and then another. Minnie sat bolt upright. She could feel the ship grinding and screaming in agony as the rocks pierced her hull.

Minnie's seasickness was forgotten as blind panic sent her scrambling from her berth. Already the water was rushing into the stateroom, but she grabbed her glasses—she had to have her glasses—and a sweater to cover her shoulders.

The sea roared in as the ship listed steeply, and without quite knowing how she got there, Minnie found herself out in the saloon, waist-deep in the icy waters that roared down over the stairs from the smoker, bringing with it the piano and other furniture, including some of the ship's railing. The sea caught her and threw her against the side of the saloon, and in the struggle against it, she lost her glasses. It was at that moment that the dynamos were flooded and the ship was plunged into darkness.

The water buffeted Minnie and kept pulling her under. It would have been so easy to give up, but the will to live kept her going. *Get up*, she told herself, *you're not going to be drowned.*

She was conscious of voices shouting and screaming above the roar of the sea and the battering of the ship. Men were hollering, "We'll be drowned like rats!" In the darkness she groped her way along the wall towards the voices. She held on and worked her way to the companionway and joined the shouting, struggling people. Then she was carried upward with the stream.

Kitty Cantwell was still awake when the *Florizel* struck. She felt the violent shock, and heard the grinding, crashing, and screaming of metal against rocks. Almost immediately came the voice of Snow, the steward, pounding on doors along the hallway. "All hands on deck— the ship's aground," he shouted. Nearer and nearer he came, until he was pounding at Kitty's stateroom. Meantime, Kitty had taken the shock calmly. She would have to dress and get her friend Annie on the move.

"Did you hear that, Annie? We'll have to dress and get out of here," she called.

Annie didn't seem to care. She lay in her berth, unmoving, and moaning softly. Outside there was chaos, people shouting, crying out. The ship quivered under the assault of the furious seas.

Kitty dressed quickly, putting on her long stylish boots, her skirt, and a coat. "Come on, Annie, we've got to get on deck," she urged.

She forced the inert young woman to a sitting position and helped her to dress—Annie was too sick to care. "Come on, now," Kitty encouraged. She forced Annie's feet into her boots and hurriedly laced them, pulled her to her feet, and into her coat.

They left their stateroom and stepped out into the hallway—up to their knees into the icy sea, and into the fighting, shouting stream of humanity. The lights went out as they stepped into the hallway, and the rushing sea took them, carried them floundering into the blackness.

Annie, shocked into realization, cried, "Kitty, don't leave me!"

Clinging to the walls and to each other, the girls were jostled around in the blackness with the sea washing around them. Men and women screamed.

Kitty grasped her friend firmly and, clinging together, they were washed along the hall by the force of water. The young woman felt only annoyance at the shouting and screaming around them. What, she thought, was the use of making all that noise? They'd be better off to save their breath.

Helpless to help themselves, they were carried here and there, beaten about the ship, with Kitty holding fast to anything her strong young arms could find. Annie, becoming stronger with the strength of desperation, clung fast to Kitty. The waves sweeping through the ship boiled around them, engulfing them.

Gasping for air, Annie cried, "Kitty! I can't go on."

But Kitty was adamant. "Come on!" And only Kitty's determination to hold on to everything—anything—kept them from being swept to their deaths.

Eventually they found themselves by a doorway, and when it wasn't buried under a cascade of water, they could see the sky was brightening. They could also see that the lifeboats and railing had been swept away.

Up in the smoker, the grey light of dawn was penetrating the blackness, and as the struggling passengers fought against being carried back over the steps, a voice called, "Is that you, Miss Denief?"

It was the voice of John Johnston, the young pantry steward.

Minnie called back, "Yes, it's me!"

She found herself beside him, saw he wore a lifebelt, and was holding shut the door leading to the deck with all his strength.

He shouted, "Grab hold of my lifebelt, and don't let go!"

Minnie grabbed and clung to him while he struggled with the door that was now being split asunder by the strength of the sea.

He shouted, "We'll have to try and get out of here."

A man and woman came toward them, and in the lightening day Minnie recognized him as a buyer in one of the big St. John's stores.

They huddled inside the door, the four of them, when a giant sea smashed on the *Florizel*, splintering great sections of her. It wrenched the door off completely and part of the smoker was torn away, exposing them to the full strength of the angry seas that roared towards them. The man and woman beside them were picked up and swept over the rail on the crest of the wave, but Minnie clung to Johnston's lifebelt.

The ship was disintegrating rapidly, and passengers and luggage disappeared in the seething, frothy seas. In the struggle for survival, forty-two people eventually reached safety, but the lives of ninety-four were lost.

Shortly after the ship struck, Captain Joe Kean was assisting with one of the lifeboats when a huge sea smashed it. Some of the wreckage of the boat hit Captain Kean and broke his leg. Alex Ledingham, Captain Martin, and Chief Officer James assisted him to the smoker with great difficulty. Other passengers were beginning to fill the room, and they laid Joe Kean on a table there. He thanked them, saying that if he hadn't broken his leg, he would have stood a chance of surviving. But when the smoker was swept away it took with it about forty people—including Captain Kean.

Daybreak. The cold light revealed naked and nearly naked people, beaten and bruised by the sea, clinging to anything their hands could find. They worked their way for'ard where the ship was still above water. Many were knocked unconscious by the impact of the waves, then swept overboard.

In the brief seconds between waves Johnston shouted to Minnie Denief, "Hold on tight and we'll try to get up forward to the Marconi room."

The deck was iced over and offered poor footing, yet they managed to inch along between the breaking seas, Johnston clinging to the railing and Minnie clinging to him.

Precipitous waves reared above them, rising in fury to their full height, then crashing to crush the ship under tons of water.

One wave lifted Minnie and carried her over the rail. Still clinging to Johnston's lifebelt, battered and nearly drowned, she hung on with no thought of releasing her grip. Miraculously, the wave broke and the water surged backwards with sufficient force to bring her over the rail again.

Now even the railing was being torn from the deck. Clinging to anything that would give him a hold, Johnston inched along the ice with Minnie clinging behind. Bodies of men and women floated by, but Minnie steeled herself to think only of hanging on to John Johnston's lifebelt.

A flagstaff crashed to the deck beside them. Then Johnston slipped and both of them lost their balance. Unable to hold on, Minnie released her grip on Johnston's lifebelt and felt herself being carried away, and she knew that this was the end, that her struggles had been in vain. Her mind accepted this in an instant. But Johnston was a quick thinker as well as a fighter. He grabbed for her, caught her by her long black hair, and clung with the other arm to the flagstaff lying along the deck. Minnie did not struggle. In this tug-of-war between man and sea she was helpless as the sea engulfed her, and she remained like this until the avalanche of water had passed. John Johnston, still holding her by the hair, pulled her back, shouting words of encouragement, trying to get her to hang on to his lifebelt once more. But Minnie was completely spent, beaten and bruised and unable to help.

The Marconi room was just ahead of them, and Johnston—apparently determined to carry out his promise to her father to look after her—transferred his grip from Minnie's long hair to her ankle, and crawling along the deck with the aid of the flagstaff, dragged her along, unresisting.

Dazed and battered, Minnie saw that she was the first passenger in the Marconi room, but that there were two wireless operators and two engineers already there. The wireless was hopelessly smashed, and the men were directing an SOS by flashlight towards the shore where a fire had been lit by people on a beach.

Too numb even to feel the cold, Minnie huddled against the wall of the tiny Marconi room, thankful for its dubious protection against the fury of the sea.

The sea advanced and withdrew, exposing the great black rocks surrounding them. It was a terrifying sight to Kitty Cantwell, but there was no time to think. Foaming streams of water raced through the ship, caught Kitty and Annie Dalton and swept them out on the sloping deck where they received the full force of the seas that seemed to tumble out of the skies on top of them. Kitty's arms found something, and she hung on. Annie was still with her, still clinging to her waist, as the wave receded. She gasped, "Kitty, don't leave me."

Kitty didn't waste any breath reassuring her friend, she was busy watching the mountain of foam towering up above them. She grabbed her friend and hung on. The salt sea stung her eyes, took her breath away, beat at her and around her, ragged at her—then it was gone.

"Kitty, I can't go on," Annie choked.

"Come on," Kitty said grimly, and before the next wave struck they had clawed their way a few feet along the deck. They pitted their puny strength time and again, slowly making their way to safety.

Annie was weakening, but suddenly there was a strong young man also fighting his way against the sea. Kitty appealed to him.

"Can you look after my friend? She's not well."

But the young man was concerned only with himself. He said no, he couldn't help. And was soon out of sight.

It seemed to her that time stood still while she and Annie fought for survival. The seas beat at them endlessly, sweeping them along, bruising their bodies, almost tearing her arms from their sockets. She learned to turn her head and hold her breath when the wall of foam swept toward them to gauge the precious seconds between batterings.

Then suddenly, about ten feet away, they saw a door. It was closed, and looked solidly safe, and Kitty was going to reach it. She took a firm grip on her friend, encouraging her toward the door. Wreckage had accumulated on the deck. Annie raised her foot to step over it. A wall of water struck at that moment. It lifted Annie off her feet and swept her over the rail in the twinkling of an eye. Kitty saw her friend disappear even as the seas engulfed her.

In that shocking moment when her friend went to her death, Kitty's brain worked clearly. To let go and try to rescue her friend meant certain death for herself, and Annie probably died instantaneously, she thought. Nothing could live in that raging, boiling hell of white water and black rocks.

So Kitty found herself alone on her hands and knees, crawling, crawling—and then she was at the door. She pounded and called to be let in. The waves were rushing at her again. Her hands found something to cling to, and she turned her back to the onrush and let the sea do its worst. But the water didn't have quite so much power here, and Kitty continued to pound on the door. She knew there were people behind it.

"Let me in," she called.

A man's voice called back, "It's all filled in here."

"Let me in!" she called again.

But she was thinking, philosophically, *if it's filled, it's filled*. She decided to remain where she was.

From inside the door, a man's voice: "It's a woman. Let her in."

There was a considerable period before the door was opened, and Kitty watched in fascination the relentless fury of the sea, watched it withdraw from the black, slimy rocks, then rush back to boil furiously and pound the ship.

The door, which had jammed, was opened, and willing hands grabbed her, drew her into the tiny Marconi room, so solidly jammed with people it was a wonder she could squeeze in.

Other survivors had fought their way to the Marconi room, crowding in until they were packed like sardines. The ex-serviceman Mullowney arrived alone, his war wounds open and bleeding. His wife and child had been lost, he said, they had been swept overboard.

Thirty-two survivors crowded into the tiny room, a precarious shelter that shivered under the onslaught of the furious seas. But it was spared annihilation by the huge smoke stack that took the brunt of the sea's fury, although the waves smashing on the roof, split the seams open, making the cramped quarters almost unbearable.

One of the survivors was fully dressed, and it was suggested that he offer his heavy overcoat to Minnie Denief, who was flimsily clad and blue with cold. The young stalwart refused point-blank.

The *Florizel*, buffeted severely and swinging to and fro on the rocks that impaled her, was threatening to break in two. Minnie was fearful that the ship would break up beneath them. She asked Johnston, "What will happen if the Marconi room breaks in half?"

He joked, "Why, you go one way and I go the other."

Mullowney bled copiously and died beside Minnie. The men put his body outside to make room for the living. Another young man began to go to pieces under the strain and was prepared to give up, but John Johnston shook him, rubbed his face, and gave cheerful words of encouragement.

Among the survivors crowding the Marconi room were Captain Martin and a seaman named William Dooley. The captain had come to the decision that nothing could be done unless they could get a line ashore. He made up his mind to attach a line to his waist and attempt to swim ashore. The survivors tried to dissuade him, saying he would only drown, to which he replied that if he did, then his body would probably wash upon the shore and rescuers would have a line.

Seaman Dooley volunteered to swim to shore with him, and both men tried to reach forward to find a rope, but the seas were too powerful and the attempt had to be abandoned.

The bitter hours passed while the seas savagely attacked the *Florizel* as though she were a plaything. Night descended and there had been no sign of rescue. The afterdeck of the once-proud liner was completely submerged. With the added misery of darkness, the survivors wondered if the world had forgotten them.

Messages, flashed earlier to St. John's, sparked rescue operations. Ships had to get up steam, crews had to be assembled, and Navy reservists from HMS *Briton* were called upon to fill in. But around midday confusing messages began to arrive from Cappahayden to the effect that there were no survivors, all lives had been lost, and *Florizel* was a total wreck.

Because of these messages, rescue operations were halted and did not continue until much later, when new messages came from Cappahayden about survivors seen on the wreck. It was late afternoon before most of the ships steamed from St. John's, and it wasn't until daybreak the following day that the ships reached the battered, broken *Florizel*.

The night had passed in misery, and dawn brought no relief. Inside the Marconi room, a man standing by the porthole could see the waves coming, and he would make the sign of the cross with his crucifix. Another man recited the rosary, while non-Catholics sang "Nearer my God to Thee."

Minnie Denief was too frightened, too numb, and too exhausted to pray, but she was impressed by the religious fervor around her. They were all standing in the same cramped positions, with no room to move an inch. Her feet were frostbitten, her body was one dull ache, and she wondered if they were ever going to be rescued.

But rescue was not far off, for as the day brightened, ships were steaming towards them. The *Terra Nova* was already hove-to close by. She had spent an hour trying to launch lifeboats, but they capsized and the men were thrown into the water.

Finally, Captain Perry of the *Gordon C* launched a dory and, with a seaman by the name of Budden, maneuvered the small boat between the ugly rocks and the wrecked liner and shouted for survivors.

The two women were the first to go. Kitty Cantwell was carried to the ship's side and told to jump. She had time to glimpse the beach and the hundreds of people watching before she obediently jumped into the little dory that rose and fell so frighteningly under the hull of the ship. Minnie Denief followed, and after an alarming journey through the surf, both were safe and snug aboard the *Gordon C*.

In the lengthy inquiry that followed, the cause for the wreck of the *Florizel* was laid to gale-force winds, ice, poor visibility, and the possibility of the Arctic current reversing itself on that particular night, thus further impeding the speed of the ship.

Captain William Martin was suspended for twenty-one months, but in view of his previous good record and general care and attention to duty, was allowed a chief mate's interim certificate for the time of suspension.

Kitty Cantwell never did get to visit her sister in New York, and never set foot on another ship. In May of that year she married Michael McDonald, and they lived on Parade Street in St. John's.

Minnie Denief sailed for New York a year later almost to the day, and though it was also a stormy trip, this time she made it safely.

She became an American citizen in due course, married Henry Krapf, and lived in Brooklyn, New York.

John Johnston was without doubt one of the outstanding heroes of the *Florizel* disaster, and so great was his modesty that he did not even testify at the hearings. His story was passed along to the public during the inquiry by Minnie Denief. He died in St. John's in 1955.

BROOMS FOR SALE
Thomas H. Raddall

This is a true story that happened many years ago. Greta was a young widow then, with a boy aged nine. They lived on a small farm in the woods west of the LaHave River, near the coast of Nova Scotia. They were very poor.

Greta did all the farm work herself, tending the cattle, ploughing, seeding, and harvesting. In winter, she got her own firewood with an axe in the woods. She was a tall Nova Scotian girl with the heart of a man. She had not the strength of a man, though, and no man lived near enough to help her. That was why the house and barn needed repair, and the fences were falling down. That was why each year the crops were smaller. But Greta would not give up.

One winter she thought of a way to get some extra money. There was a fishing village towards the mouth of the LaHave, not many miles away. When the fishermen fitted out their vessels each spring, they needed all sorts of things. One thing was a supply of good brooms—but not the kind you buy in the shops. Fishermen must have a very stiff and strong broom, to sweep the deck after cutting and cleaning the day's catch.

Greta had grown up in a shore village and had seen such things made. You take a stick of birch wood about four feet long and three or four inches thick. Then you take a good strong jackknife. First, you must remove the birchbark. Then you start at one end of the stick, cutting a splint or shaving about half an inch wide and about as thick as the knife blade. You keep pushing the knife blade within eight inches of the other end. There you stop. You go back and start another splint. You keep doing that, round and round the stick, until it is no more than an inch and a half thick. And there is your broom handle.

Now you take the bush of splints hanging near the other end, and bend them back over the eight inches of solid wood remaining there. You bind them together tightly in that position with strong cod line, and with an axe you cut them off at about twelve inches below the cord. And there is your broom, all in one piece.

The Bank Fleet was very large in those days, and in the course of a season each vessel used a number of brooms. So each winter the outfitters bought a good supply.

Greta decided to make some brooms. The days were short and there were many chores to do in the house and barn, not to mention the woodpile. She would have to do this extra chore after dark. The whittling made such a mess in her clean kitchen that she took part of the barn for a workshop.

Every evening after supper, when the little boy was asleep, she went to the barn, lit a fire in a rusty tin stove, and sat there hour after hour cutting splints by the light of the lantern. Her hands were used to hard work, but after a time the grip on the knife made them sore. She tried wearing gloves, but that was awkward. So she tied a strip of linen over the blisters and went on. What pain she suffered, you can guess. But at last her palms were rough and hard, and she could work without a bandage. Sometimes she made four or five brooms before midnight.

By the end of January she had two hundred and forty brooms. It was time to sell them.

One chilly morning in February, Greta hitched the mare Judy to the sleigh and loaded her brooms. She helped her child into the seat, and started for West LaHave. She left the boy in the care of her nearest neighbours, three miles down the road. It was pleasant driving through the woods, with the runners creaking on the snow and the harness bells ringing.

The village appeared, with its wharves and stores, and the wide frozen surface of the river. Greta got out of the sleigh happily. But in the first store she had disappointing news. The ship outfitters at West LaHave had a full stock of brooms. They could buy no more.

"You might sell them down the river at East LaHave," a storekeeper said, pointing over the ice. Greta looked. In the clear winter air the river did not seem very wide—half a mile, say. And three miles down the east shore was a chance to sell her precious brooms.

"The ice is good," the man said. "Several teams have been across today."

So Greta headed the mare across the river. It was pretty, she said afterwards: ice on the broad stream as far as you could see; the white banks and the dark woods; blue smoke rising in wisps from the houses by the shore.

When she reached East LaHave she was stiff from the long drive in the cold, but she entered the store with a quick step and an eager face. The storekeeper looked out at her load and shook his head.

"Sorry, Lady, but it seems everybody's been making brooms this winter. We've got too many now."

Half a dozen fishing captains sat by the store, smoking and talking over the coming season on the Banks. They looked at the woman from up the river. Her coat was cheap and old, too thin for this sort of weather. They saw the worn overshoes, the home-knit woolen cap, the hands twisting anxiously inside the grey mittens. They looked at her tight mouth, and her eyes holding back the tears.

One of them said quietly, "Buy her brooms. If you don't, we will." The storekeeper called one of his clerks to carry the brooms inside. They made a great heap on the floor.

"Let's see, now. Two hundred and forty brooms at twenty-five cents...."

"Forty cents," the fishing captain said. "Those are good brooms. I'd say you made them yourself, didn't you, ma'am?"

"Yes," Greta said.

The storekeeper counted out ninety-six dollars—nine tens, a five, and a one. Greta thanked him and the captain in a small, choked voice. As she went out the door one of them said, "You'd better drive home smart, ma'am. Looks like snow." She noticed then that the sunshine was gone and the sky was filled with a grey scud coming in very fast from the sea. A bleak, uneasy wind was blowing this way and that.

Greta had no purse. She stopped and fastened the banknotes to the inside hem of her skirt, using a big safety pin. She drove off, humming a tune to herself and thinking of the things she could buy now for her boy and for the farm. Before she had gone far, the snow began to fly in small hard specks. When she reached to the crossing place, a blizzard was blowing. She could not see across the river.

She turned off the road onto the ice, following the faint tracks of the other teams. After ten minutes the old tracks disappeared, buried in the new snow sweeping along the ice. She had to trust the horse to find the way. Greta was not afraid. After all, it was only half a mile or so.

The snow was now so thick that she could not see past Judy's ears. She let the reins go slack and crouched down in the seat trying to find a little comfort in the storm. There was none. The snow whirled and stung; it seemed to come from every side. Sometimes it stopped her breath, like a cold white cloth laid over her mouth and nose. The little mare kept plunging her head and snorting in the blasts.

The way seemed strangely long. Greta noticed the light was growing dim. The afternoon had gone. Soon now, surely she must see the west shore looming through the storm. The horse went on and on, slipping here and there on patches of bare ice.

At last Judy came to a stop. Greta peered into the swirling snow and saw a dim, pale shape ahead. She shielded her eyes with her mittened hand for a better look. Through the snow gusts she could see the thing was large, with three slim objects standing upon it reaching up into the murk. Trees, of course!

"Good girl, Judy! There's the shore. I knew you'd find it."

She urged the horse on with a jerk at the reins. Judy went on a few steps and stopped again. The object stretched right across her path. It was close and clear now, and Greta gasped. Her very heart seemed to stop beating. For there, like a ghost risen out of the ice, lay a ship. A ship, of all things. A big schooner with three tall masts, all crusted with snow. What was it doing there? Slowly her mind filled with an awful suspicion. She tried to put it aside, but it came back. At last she faced the truth.

The little mare had been lost all this time. Instead of crossing the ice, they had been wandering down the river, towards the open sea. They were now somewhere near the mouth, where the ice was never safe. To prove it, here was the big three-master frozen in where the crew had left it moored for the winter.

Poor Greta's heart was beating again in slow hard thumps. She was frightened. She did not know which way to turn. Were vessels anchored with their bows upstream or down? Or were they just moored any way at all? She could not remember.

It was quite dark now. Greta's arms and legs felt numb. One thing was certain, she was freezing there in the bitter wind and snow. So was the little horse. They must move or perish. Greta made up her mind. She got down and took hold of Judy's bridle, turned the sleigh carefully, and began to walk, leading the horse straight away from the long, pointing bowsprit of the schooner.

The strongest blasts of the storm seemed to come from the right. Greta kept the wind on her right cheek. In that way at least she would avoid moving in a circle.

Suppose the wind changes? asked a small cold voice inside her. But that was the voice of feat, and she refused to listen.

The effort of walking took some of the cold ache out of Greta's legs, but there was no feeling in her hands and feet, and her cheeks felt like wood. She kept changing her hold on Judy's bridle and rubbing her face with the other hand. The storm tore at her long full skirt and darted icy fingers through her thin coat. The world seemed full of snow, driving in a sharp slant on the wind, and sweeping along the ice with a hiss like escaping stream.

The mare was not shod for this sort of footing. She slipped and stumbled and seemed very tired. Greta herself felt weary and empty. She had eaten nothing since the hasty breakfast at the farm. Sometimes the wind lulled, and the cloud of fine snow drifted slowly about them. Its touch then was soft upon the cheek. Greta was tempted to let Judy go, to lie down on the ice and let that cold white power go on brushing her face and soothing her fears and worries. Somehow the snow made her think of bedsheets, clean and cool to the skin. How nice it would be, just to lie down and sleep away the night!

But whenever Greta's eyes closed and the strength seemed to flow out of her limbs, there came into her mind a picture of the lonely boy at the neighbour's house, with his nose against the glass. She opened her eyes then, and stepped forward strongly in the darkness.

As the night went on, this happened many times. Greta became more and more drowsy with the cold, and more weary. The little horse lagged and stumbled worse and worse. Finally, after one of those dreamy pauses, as Greta began to lead the horse again, she came upon a black patch in the ice ahead. It extended to the right and left as far as she could see. She moved closer—and stepped back in alarm. It was water—open water. She could hear it lapping against the edge of the ice.

She thought, *This is the end. We have come to the sea.*

She closed her eyes, praying slowly and silently. She stood there a long time. At last she put her chin up. Aloud she said, "Judy, it's all or nothing now. Suppose it isn't the sea—suppose it's just the flooded ice along the shore! You know, where the ice sinks and buckles when the tide falls down the river. There's only one way to prove it, Judy. I must go to the edge and let my feet down into the water. Come, girl? Steady now! Come!"

Greta led the mare to the edge of the ice. The water looked very black. The snow was blowing harder than ever.

If only I could see, she thought, *just for a minute. Just for a second. If only I could be sure.* But there was only one way to be sure in this stormy blackness. She took a turn of the reins about her wrist, stooped, and lowered her left foot into the water. It came to her ankle, to her knee. The cold grip of the water sent pain to her very bones. She gasped and lost her balance.

For one wild moment Greta thought she was gone. The sea! She was plunging into the sea! But her feet came upon something now, something slippery but solid. It was the sunken ice. She was standing over her knees in water. She paused to gather courage and her breath. She waded out to the length of the reins. The flooded ice held firm. It was tilted against hidden rocks, and now the water barely reached her trembling knees.

"Come, Judy," she cried, and pulled on the reins. The mare snorted and would not more. Greta threw her whole weight on the reins. Judy tried to draw back, but her worn iron shoes had no grip on the ice. Snorting with fear, she was dragged over the edge into the water. Greta found herself being dragged over the edge into the water. Greta found herself being dragged by the reins about her hand.

The horse had floundered past her. She caught hold on the lurching sleigh. Dimly she saw a solid whiteness looming out of the windy dark. It was the shore—a pasture deep in snow.

Greta took the mare's head and led her up the bank. There was a low fence. The poles were rotten and she broke them down. She led Judy along inside the fence, wading through the drifts until she came to a gate and saw a light. Then she was standing at Judy's head outside a house and crying for help.

A man and a woman came to the door. She cried again, and they ran out to her. The man unhitched Judy quickly and took her off to the warmth and shelter of his barn. The woman half-led, half-carried Greta into her kitchen. Greta's clothes were crusted with snow, her wet skirts frozen stiff. But before she would let the good woman do anything for her, she stooped and turned up the icy hem of her skirt.

The precious packet was still there. She counted the notes with her numb white fingers. She laughed shakily. It was all there, the money she had made with her own hands, the money she had saved by her own courage in the storm.

ABOUT THE CONTRIBUTORS

David Abbass, born and brought up in Halifax, launched his hockey career in 1964 on Arnold Sarty's rink next door on Hemlock Street. When the Sarty's lawn died, he was traded to Bill Butler's rink up the road before breaking into the Halifax recreation league. He is still paying his dues in hobby leagues in Germany, where he lives with his wife, Mitzi, and their three sons, Nicholas, Thomas, and Lucas. His quest to be the oldest rookie in the NHL is self-funded, with stints as reporter and editor for the *Chronicle Herald* and the *Mail-Star*, communications specialist and science writer-editor in Asia and the Middle East, and, his current post, communications officer with the United Nations Climate Change Secretariat in Bonn.

Greta Gaskin Bidlake (1890–1969) grew up in Coverdale, New Brunswick, on a farm overlooking the Petitcodiac River. Today the old Gaskin property is home to the Riverview Town Hall. Both her husband and brother perished in the First World War and Greta taught school for many years, writing a memoir of her experiences teaching in Labrador. She wrote many children's stories that were published in United Church publications. She also wrote for *Saturday Night*, *Family Herald*, and the *Weekly Star*.

Cassie Brown (1919–1986) was born in Rose Blanche, Newfoundland, and moved with her family to St. John's in the 1930s. She was a journalist, author, editor, and publisher throughout her career and published her most distinguished book, *Death on the Ice*, in 1972.

Scott Cunningham is the author of *Sea Kayaking in Nova Scotia*, and in 1980, managed to circumnavigate Nova Scotia in an open canoe. Scott and his partner, Gayle Wilson, offer sea kayaking tours throughout Atlantic Canada from their base on Nova Scotia's eastern shore.

Wayne Curtis is a Miramichi writer, storyteller, and fishing guide living in Fredericton, New Brunswick. He has written numerous books including Long Ago and Far Away: A Miramichi Family Memoir and River Stories. You can find him online at waynecurtis.ca.

Monica Graham is a writer and journalist. She is the author of numerous nonfiction books including *The Great Maritime Detective*, *Fire Spook: the Mysterious Nova Scotia Haunting*, *In the Spirit*, and *Bluenose*. She lives in Pictou County, Nova Scotia.

Michael Francis Harrington (1916–1999) was born in St. John's and worked in publishing, writing, and broadcasting. He was the editor in chief at the *Telegram* for more than two decades and was also active in politics both before and after Newfoundland joined Confederation. He wrote a number of books and received the Order of Canada as well as an honorary doctorate from Memorial University.

Sara Jewell is the author of *Field Notes: A City's Girl Search for Heart and Home in Rural Nova Scotia*, published by Nimbus in 2016, and writes a biweekly column for the *Citizen-Record*. She lives along the River Philip near Oxford, Nova Scotia. Visit her online at sarajewell.ca.

Stephen Abbass lives with his wife in Dartmouth, Nova Scotia. When not mowing the lawn or shovelling snow, he can generally be found at a local coffee shop with a learned group of friends. A long time denizen of the theatre, Stephen has penned numerous works for the stage including his musical play *Best Friends*.

Jim Lutes has had a long and successful career in financial management that has taken him around the world. He is currently leading Private Company Transaction Advisory Services for Canada at Ernst & Young. Jim lives in Rothesay, New Brunswick, and is an avid cyclist and fly fisherman, and spends as much time as he can outdoors in all seasons.

Alistair MacLeod (1936–2014) was born in Saskatchewan and moved with his family to a farm in Cape Breton at the age of ten. Considered one of Canada's greatest writers, his works include *The Lost Salt Gift of Blood*, *As Birds Bring Forth the Sun and Other Stories*, and *No Great Mischief*, which won the prestigious International DUBLIN Literary Award in 2001.

Archibald MacMechan (1862–1933) was a graduate of University of Toronto who taught English at Dalhousie University in Halifax for forty years. He wrote classic sea tales from the age of sail including *Sagas of the Sea* and *There Go the Ships*. He was described by Thomas Raddall as "an erect and dignified figure with a grey torpedo beard," and, perhaps more than any other Canadian writer, crafted stirring seafaring stories. Archibald MacMechan also served as the official historian for the Halifax Explosion Relief Commission.

Norma Jean MacPhee is a creative and enthusiastic writer and journalist from Cape Breton. With over a decade of experience across many platforms, she possesses a genuine interest in people, their stories, and the health of communities. Her first fiction short story, "Silence the Soundtrack," was published in the anthology *Thirteen Ways from Sunday*.

One of Canada's most distinguished poets, Nova Scotia's **Alden Nowlan** (1933–1983) is also one of the country's most enduring novelists and short story writers. His works include *Will ye let the Mummers in?*, *The Wanton Troopers*, and *Bread, Wine and Salt*, which won the 1967 Governor General's Award for poetry.

Michael O. Nowlan was born in Chatham, New Brunswick. He spent thirty-five years as a schoolteacher, most of them in Oromocto, where he has lived since 1964. He has edited or written more than twenty books including *Ole Larson's Miramichi*, the poetry collection *The Other Side*, and the Christmas anthology *The Last Bell*.

Harry G. Paddon was born and brought up in Labrador where his father was a medical missionary. He returned to Labrador after completing his formal education and became a trapper as well as a pioneer doctor. He wrote *Labrador Doctor: My Life With the Grenfell Mission* and his account of travelling by dog team during the winter of 1947, certainly stands as one of the seminal accounts of life in Canada's north.

Tom Pond first went to work in the Miramichi lumber camps in the 1920s at the age of fifteen. As a boy, he heard many of the old Dungarvon Whooper legends being told by the old-timers in the camps, and spent many springs watching the great river unload its ice flows while the log river drives were in full swing.

One of Nova Scotia's most loved storytellers, **Thomas H. Raddall** (1903 –1994) won the Governor General's Literary Award three times. He is the author of numerous books including *Halifax: Warden of the North*, *Hangman's Beach*, *The Nymph and the Lamp*, and *His Majesty's Yankees*.

Saint John's **W. E. Daniel (Dan) Ross** (1912–1995) was a bestselling novelist with over three hundred books to his credit. His wife, Charlotte, sometimes assisted him, and he wrote in a variety of genres, including gothic fiction, and used a number of pseudonyms including Marilyn Ross.

Gary Saunders was born and raised in Newfoundland and is a long-time resident of Nova Scotia. Gary is an artist and naturalist, and has published a range of nonfiction titles, including *Trees of Nova Scotia*, *Discover Nova Scotia: The Ultimate Nature Guide*, and the childhood memoir *Free Wind Home*.

A. R. (Arthur) Scammell (1913–1995) was a major cultural figure in twentieth-century Newfoundland and Labrador. Born in Notre Dame Bay, Scammell wrote the enduring ballad "Squid Jiggin' Grounds" and was named to the Order of Canada in 1988.

Paul Skerry is a Halifax-based architect, writer, and adventure traveller. From Costa Rica and Vietnam, through Africa and the highest peaks of the Andes, he has travelled the globe in search of the unusual and the exotic. When not travelling or working twenty-four-seven, Paul can be found luxuriating on the remote beaches and in the deep woods of the Maritimes.

Steve Vernon is one of Canada's premier storytellers. He has published numerous books and short stories for kids and adults including *Maritime Murder*, *Halifax Haunts*, and *The Lunenburg Werewolf and Other Stories from the Supernatural*. He lives in Halifax, Nova Scotia.

PUBLICATION CREDITS

Stories not listed here were either originally published by Nimbus, not previously published, or are now in the public domain.

Brown, Cassie. "A Winter's Tale." Reproduced by permission of the Estate of Cassie Brown.

MacLeod, Alistair. "Winter Dog." Excerpted from *As Birds Bring Forth the Sun and Other Stories* by Alistair MacLeod. Copyright © 1986 Alistair MacLeod. Reprinted by permission of McClelland and Stewart, a division of Penguin Random House Canada Limited.

Raddall, Thomas H. "Brooms for Sale." Courtesy of the Thomas Raddall fonds (MS-2-202), Dalhousie University Archives, Halifax, Nova Scotia.

The following stories were originally published in various issues of Atlantic Advocate, *which is now owned by Brunswick News Inc. Reproduced by permission of Jamie Irving and Brunswick News Inc.:*

Cunningham, Scott. "Skiing Across the Highlands."
Harrington, Michael Francis. "When the Reindeer Came to Newfoundland."
Nowlan, Michael. "One Special Present."
Pond, Tom. "The Ice Run."
Ross, Charlotte and Dan. "Christmas Eve Call."
Saunders, Gary. "Ice Magic."
Scammell, A. R. "Square Beam."

MORE HOLIDAY BOOKS
FROM NIMBUS

The Christmas Secret
ISBN: 9781551099330

To Every Thing
There is a Season
ISBN: 9781551099439

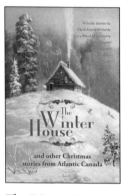

The Winter House
ISBN: 9781551098623

An Atlantic Canadian
Christmas Reader
ISBN: 9781551097855

Vintage Christmas
ISBN: 9781771084505

The Finest Tree
ISBN: 9781771081702